ASK THE QUESTION

UNLOCKING YOUR POTENTIAL
THROUGH PLAYFUL CURIOSITY

ISBN: 978-1-971349-53-4

For Kat, I hope you always stay endlessly curious.

Table of Contents

INTRODUCTION

Here's a bold truth you probably already feel in your bones:

The quality of your life is not shaped by the answers you collect — it is shaped by the questions you are brave enough to ask.

Think about it. Every breakthrough you've ever had — in your career, your relationships, your money, your identity — began with a question. Sometimes it was quiet. Sometimes it was messy. Sometimes it felt risky. But it was always the question that moved you forward.

This book exists because most of us were trained to stop asking.

As kids, we were born curious — asking *why* a hundred times before breakfast. But somewhere along the way, the world taught us that curiosity was inconvenient, disruptive, or "too much." We learned to perform instead of wonder, comply instead of question, and fit in instead of think freely.

And in the process, we lost access to one of our greatest superpowers.

I've spent my career — first in law, then in finance, and now as the founder of **PBJ Mortgage** and **Financial Mastery Simplified** — watching what happens when people are afraid to ask the right questions about their money, their choices, and their lives.

In mortgages, I've seen brilliant, capable people stay stuck simply because they were afraid to say:

"I don't understand — can you explain that?"

In personal finance, I've watched women do everything "right" and still feel trapped because they never asked:

"Is this actually aligned with what I want?"

And in my own life, everything changed the moment I asked one disruptive, playful, life-altering question:

"What if getting a mortgage could feel as simple as making a peanut butter and jelly sandwich?"

That question didn't just create a brand. It created a movement.

It became the foundation of **PBJ Mortgage — where mortgages are human, simple, and empowering, not intimidating and shame-based.** It also became the heartbeat of **Financial Mastery Simplified — where we help women rewrite their money stories, trust their instincts, and design a financial life that works on their terms.**

Here's what I've learned:

You don't need more answers.
You need better questions.

This book is not here to tell you what to think. It is here to teach you how to ask.

Over these pages, you'll explore:

- How curiosity rewires your brain and expands your power
- Why fear shuts down your voice — and how to reclaim it
- How systems train us to comply instead of question
- How to ask for what you want without guilt or shame

- How to use questions to unlock clarity, confidence, and purpose
- And how one bold question can completely change your life

You will be invited to pause, reflect, and — most importantly — practice. Because curiosity isn't something you find. It's a muscle you build.

By the end of this book, my hope is simple but powerful:

You will stop waiting for permission.
You will trust your instincts again.
And you will remember that your voice matters.

Because the future does not belong to the people with all the answers.

It belongs to the people who dare to ask better questions.

And that future? It starts now.

Welcome in.

— Jacqueline "Jax" Crider
Founder, PBJ Mortgage
Creator, Financial Mastery Simplified

CHAPTER I

The Power of Asking Questions

*"Curiosity is the spark behind every great idea.
The future belongs to the curious."*
— Anonymous

Let's take it back for a second.

You remember when your favorite word was why, right?

As a kid, it came out of your mouth nonstop. Why is the sky blue? Why do I have to go to bed now? Why can't dogs talk? You were curious about everything—bold, playful, relentless.

And honestly? That curiosity was powerful. It was how you learned, how you explored, how you connected with the world.

But somewhere along the way, the questions started fading.

Not because you stopped being curious, but because you were told—directly or indirectly—that asking too many questions was annoying, naive, or disruptive.

Maybe it was a teacher who called on someone else instead of you.
Maybe it was a boss who said, "Just trust the process."
Maybe it was a parent, trying their best, who said, "Because I said so."

And so, like so many of us, you stopped asking

The Real Superpower Nobody Talks About

Let me say this as clearly as I can:

Your ability to ask the right question is a **superpower**.

Not a soft skill. Not a nice personality trait. A real-deal, world-shifting superpower.

It's the one thing that can crack a closed door wide open.
The thing that turns "I'm stuck" into "I'm in motion."
That flips you from autopilot into alignment.
From surviving to expanding.

You don't need a perfect plan. You don't need to know all the steps.
You just need a better question.

Because asking the right question at the right time in the right way?
That's what sparks the stuff that actually matters:

- Clarity
- Creativity
- Courage
- Change

It's how people start companies.
How movements begin.
How relationships deepen.
How lives turn around.

And yet—most people never learn how to do it.
Or worse, they learn to stop doing it altogether.

Why?
Because we've been trained to chase answers.
To memorize, to follow rules, to get it right.

Not to wonder. Not to play. Not to sit in the question and let it lead us somewhere new.

But here's the truth that flips the whole thing on its head:

> You don't have to have all the answers.
> You just need the guts to ask better questions.

Questions like:

- "What if this isn't the only way?"
- "What's possible that I haven't even considered yet?"
- "Whose rule is this, and do I even believe it?"

Those aren't just nice journal prompts. They're pattern-breakers.
They disrupt the mental loops that keep you stuck.
They shift your energy.
They invite something fresh to the table.

And your brain? It loves that.

This isn't just motivational fluff. This is neuroscience.
When you ask a powerful question, your brain gets to work.
It starts scanning, problem-solving, connecting dots in ways it wasn't a second ago.

Let's zoom in for a second on why this works.

There's a system in your brain called the **Reticular Activating System**—RAS for short.
It's basically your mind's version of Google.

Except instead of scanning the web, it scans your life—your environment, your memories, your opportunities, your attention.

And it takes its search cues from you.

So when you ask a question like,

> "Why do I always mess this up?"
> Your RAS hears that and says, "You got it, boss!"
> And it pulls up every past failure, every moment of self-doubt, every cringe memory you've filed away since third grade.

It's not because your brain hates you—it's just doing what you told it to do.
Answer the question. Find the proof. Return the search results.

But ask a better question?

Ask:

> "What's a new way I could approach this?"

Or:

> "What might this challenge be trying to teach me?"
> Or even:
> "What would this look like if it were easy?"

And suddenly...

- New connections form.
- New energy flows in.
- Your brain starts lighting up like a pinball machine of possibility.

Because now your RAS is working in your favor, not against you.

It starts scanning for inspiration, creative angles, past wins, and fresh strategies.
You literally start seeing what you were blind to before.

It's not magic.
It's **biology + intention**.

And once you understand how to work with your brain instead of defaulting to self-sabotaging questions, the game changes.

Think about it like this:
If your thoughts are the input, your life is the output.
And your questions are the keyboard.

So if you're typing in garbage?
Guess what the results look like.

But if you start typing in better prompts?
Your brain—your internal Google—starts showing you a whole different page.

And that's the beauty of this entire book.

We're not trying to hand you pre-made answers.
We're here to train your brain to ask better questions—on purpose.
Because once you know how to do that? You can create better outcomes in any area of your life.

Business. Relationships. Confidence. Peace.
Whatever you're hungry for—curiosity is the key that unlocks it.

Here's a story to illustrate that point.

The PBJ Question That Changed Everything

Here's the thing: I've always loved the mortgage world.

I love the complexity of the numbers—the way all the moving parts come together like a puzzle.
I love the strategy, the problem-solving, the chance to walk someone through one of the biggest, most life-changing

decisions they'll ever make.
There's real power in that. It's not just paperwork—it's someone's future.

But even though I loved the work... I didn't love how I was expected to do it.

The traditional rules of the industry just never sat right with me.
The stiff language. The sterile scripts. The one-size-fits-all approach that treated people like transactions instead of humans.

It felt like creativity had been outlawed.
Joy was optional—if not actively discouraged.
And every time I tried to bring in a fresh idea or a more personal approach, it was met with a version of:
"That's not how we do it."

I hated that.

Not the work. Not the mission.
But the box it all had to fit into.

And then came this moment—one of those "line in the sand" moments I didn't see coming.

I was sitting at a mastermind event, surrounded by other entrepreneurs and leaders.
We were talking about alignment, purpose, highest and best use.
And someone asked a question that stopped me cold:

"What wakes you up? Like really wakes you up?"

I didn't have a polished answer.
But what came up was this deep knowing that something had to change.

I couldn't keep showing up the same way, following rules I didn't believe in, shrinking myself to fit someone else's blueprint.

So I started doing what I do best: I got curious.

I started asking myself real questions.
Not the safe ones like, "How do I hit my next goal?"
But the deep, permission-giving ones like:

- "What if I threw out the script?"
- "What if people actually felt good during this process?"
- "What if getting a mortgage could feel... fun?"

And then—half in play, half in rebellion—I asked myself the question that changed everything:

> "What if getting a mortgage could feel as simple as making a peanut butter and jelly sandwich?"

I laughed when I said it. I mean, who compares amortization schedules to PBJ?

But in that moment, something cracked open.

That question flipped the entire frame.

It reminded me that clarity can be simple. That financial empowerment should be accessible. That guidance can feel like a conversation, not a lecture. That this whole thing can be both smart and human.

That question became the foundation for PBJ Mortgage.

It became my lens, my litmus test, my through-line.

Every time I built something—an email, a client experience, a course—I asked:

> "Does this feel like PBJ? Is it clear, simple, satisfying, real?"

And you know what?
It attracted people who felt the same way.
People who wanted someone who would see them, teach them, and walk with them.
People who were smart and capable but just needed the process demystified.

PBJ Mortgage was born from curiosity.
Not a business plan. Not a marketing funnel.
A question.

And that's what I want you to know:

> The right question doesn't just change how you think. It can change your life.
> It can become the seed of something bigger—a new way of doing business, showing up, or being in the world.

All you have to do is ask.

Real Talk: Questions Literally Change Your Brain

That one PBJ question?

It wasn't just a clever brand hook or a cute idea.

It literally rewired how I thought.

And that's not just a metaphor. That's biology.

When you ask a question that lights you up—a question that challenges your norms, opens your perspective, or taps into something deeply true—your brain responds.

Dopamine floods in. That's your "let's go" chemical. It fuels motivation and forward motion.

New neural pathways form. This is neuroplasticity in action—your brain creating fresh connections instead of replaying the same old loops.

You shift into creative, solution-focused thinking. You stop spiraling and start building.

Translation?

> You don't just think differently—
> You become different.

This is why we're not here to hand you the "answers."

Because the truth is, most of the answers you need?
They're already inside you.
They just haven't been invited out by the right question.

That's what this book is about.

Giving you a better set of questions.
Ones that wake you up.
Ones that open doors.
Ones that help you remember who you are and what you're here to do.

Try This: Activate Your Curiosity

Let's try it right now. Seriously.

Grab your phone, open the notes app. Or get a sticky note, a napkin—whatever's handy.

Think of one area in your life that feels stuck, disconnected, or just... meh.

Don't overthink it. Just pick one.

Now ask yourself:

> What's a question I haven't dared to ask myself here?

Go big. Go bold. Go real.

Here are a few examples to jumpstart your thinking:

- Instead of: "How do I fix this?"
  → Try: "What would feel wildly aligned instead?"
- Instead of: "Why is this so hard?"
  → Try: "What would it look like if this were easy?"
- Instead of: "What's the responsible choice?"
  → Try: "What's the most honest choice?"

Then—write it down. Sit with it. Let it breathe.
Don't rush to solve it. Let the question hang out with you.

Because sometimes, just sitting with a better question is the first step.

And who knows?

That one question—maybe even one that sounds a little silly, like PBJ-level silly—could be the very thing that unlocks something big.

So go ahead. Ask it.

And see where it leads.

Where We're Headed

You were born curious.

That hasn't changed.

Even if the world tried to talk you out of it.
Even if someone once rolled their eyes at your "too many questions."
Even if you've gotten used to playing it safe, keeping it quiet, coloring inside the lines.

That spark—the one that made you ask why, what if, and why not—it's still in there.

Waiting.

And in these pages, we're going to bring it back to life.

Not by trying to be perfect.
Not by chasing someone else's formula.
But by getting real, getting playful, and learning to ask the kinds of questions that make everything feel possible again.

Because here's the truth:
Curiosity isn't a personality trait. It's a practice.
Something you can cultivate. Strengthen. Use.

Every. Single. Day.

To get unstuck.
To create.
To connect more deeply.
To come home to yourself.

And the best part?

You don't need permission.
You just need to ask.

This is your permission slip.
To wonder.
To explore.
To make it weird, make it fun, make it yours.

Because the future?
It doesn't belong to the ones with the cleanest resumes or the flashiest answers.

The future belongs to the curious.

And you, my friend, are just getting started.

CHAPTER II

The Questioning Mindset

"It's not that I'm so smart, it's just that I stay with problems longer." — **Albert Einstein**

A. Cultivating Curiosity Through Play

Let's get one thing straight: Curiosity doesn't thrive under pressure.

It doesn't show up when you're white-knuckling your way through a task list or trying to impress someone with how much you know.

Curiosity—real, open-hearted, generative curiosity—needs room to play.

Yup. I said it.
Play.

And before your inner adult rolls their eyes, hear me out.

Play isn't childish. It's essential.
Play is how we test ideas, discover connections, and stretch beyond what we think we know.

Play is where creativity, courage, and curiosity all meet up and say, "Let's try something new."

Remember When You Were a Kid?

You didn't wait for permission to ask "Why?"
You weren't embarrassed to wonder out loud or make

something up just to see how it felt.
You didn't need a strategy. You just explored.

- You made potions out of shampoo and glitter.
- You tried to build a parachute out of a trash bag and jump off the porch (...just me?).
- You asked wild questions like, "Do ants sleep?" and "What if the moon is just a giant marshmallow?"

That version of you? Got it.
Curiosity was the game. Wonder was the reward.

But somewhere between math tests, performance reviews, and "being productive," play got labeled as irresponsible. Silly. A waste of time.

And guess what? That mindset kills curiosity.

Because when everything has to be correct, efficient, and outcome-driven, there's no space to explore without judgment. No room to try, to mess up, to ask a question that might sound "dumb" but actually opens a door.

Curiosity Loves Playful Environments

If you want to think more creatively, feel more energized, and ask better questions—you've got to get playful again.

Here's what that looks like in real life:

- Trying an idea just to see what happens, not because you're sure it'll "work."
- Asking "What if?" without immediately needing an answer.
- Getting curious about something that has nothing to do with your job or your goals—just because it interests you.

- Using humor, metaphors, or absurdity to spark new thinking.

This is why I love the PBJ metaphor. It's playful. It's disarming. And it unlocks a way of thinking about mortgages (and life) that's approachable and fun.

When you bring play into your questioning, you shake off the pressure to be right and step into the power of simply wondering.

A Little Weirdness Goes a Long Way

Some of the best questions I've ever asked started out sounding... well, ridiculous.

- "What if mortgages were more like sandwiches?"
- "What would happen if I stopped marketing like a mortgage broker and started teaching like a 5th-grade science teacher?"
- "What would this look like if it were easy, fun, and radically honest?"

Those questions didn't come from a business textbook. They came from letting my brain wander by giving myself permission to play with ideas, language, and possibilities.

And every time I did? I found something worth chasing.

Try This: The Playground Prompt

Pick something in your life that feels heavy or serious right now.
A big decision. A work project. A conversation you've been avoiding.

Now, ask yourself:

What would this look like if it were a game?

What's the most playful way I could approach this?
If a six-year-old looked at this, what question would they ask?

Let yourself play with it.

No pressure. No filter. Just wonder.

Here's the bottom line:

Curiosity isn't fueled by control. It's fueled by freedom.

And the more you let yourself play, the more powerful your questions—and your answers—will become.

B. Overcoming the Fear of Asking by Embracing Playfulness

Let's be honest: Asking questions can feel scary.

Not just the big, life-altering ones like "Should I quit this job?" or "Am I really happy here?"
Even the small ones—"What do you mean by that?" or "Can you help me understand?"—can bring up a whole wave of hesitation.

Why?

Because underneath the act of asking... there's vulnerability.

When we ask a question, we're admitting we don't know something.
We're opening ourselves up to judgment. To being seen.
To possibly hearing something uncomfortable or inconvenient.

And that can be scary as hell.

Especially if you've ever been shut down, embarrassed, ignored, or told you were "too much" for being curious.

So what do we do?

We default to playing it safe.
We stay quiet.
We nod like we understand when we don't.
We let opportunities slide because asking feels like too big a risk.

But here's the thing:
Fear kills curiosity.
And the antidote?
Not more perfection. Not more preparation.

It's playfulness.

When It's Light, It's Easier to Lift

Playfulness doesn't mean not caring.
It means not over-carrying the weight of it all.

When you approach a question with curiosity instead of self-judgment, the fear gets softer.
It becomes something you can work with instead of something that paralyzes you.

Because when we treat questions like high-stakes exams, we freak ourselves out.
But when we treat questions like invitations to explore, we get bold again.

Here's what I've learned:
You don't overcome fear by trying to muscle through it.
You overcome fear by loosening your grip and letting curiosity lead the way.

Make the Question Smaller

One of my favorite tricks?

Make the question smaller. Make it fun. Make it weird, even.

Let's say you're afraid to ask someone for feedback.

Instead of framing it like:

> "Can you tell me everything that's wrong with how I
> handled this project?"
> (which—yeah, terrifying)

Try:

> "Hey, I'm experimenting with getting better at this—
> what's one thing I could tweak next time?"

Boom. Less pressure. More play.
Same goal. Different vibe.

Playfulness doesn't make the question less powerful.
It just makes it more askable.

The Voice in Your Head is Not the Boss of You

Let's talk about that little voice in your head—the one that
says:

- "This is a dumb question."
- "You should already know this."
- "If you ask this, they'll think you're
  weak/annoying/incompetent."

That voice?

Not your truth.
It's just an echo.

An old recording from some classroom, boardroom, or conversation where curiosity wasn't safe.

But you're not in that space anymore.

You're here. You're growing.
You're building a new relationship with your questions.
One where playfulness turns down the volume on fear.

Try This: Ask Like a Kid Again

Think about a question you've been afraid to ask. One that feels heavy. Loaded. Awkward.

Now imagine a seven-year-old asking it.
Imagine the wide-eyed, snack-covered energy of a kid who's just genuinely wondering.

No fear. Just play.

Rewrite your question through that lens.

For example:

- Instead of: "Am I failing at this?"
  → "What's one thing I could do differently tomorrow just to see what happens?"
- Instead of: "What if they judge me?"
  → "What if they're secretly wondering the same thing and are just too scared to ask?"

The question is the same.
But the tone? The energy? The access point?

Completely different.

You're Allowed to Ask. You're Allowed to Not Know.

Let this be your reminder:
You don't have to be perfect to ask.

You don't have to have it all figured out.
You're allowed to not know something and still be powerful.

In fact, the people who grow the fastest are the ones who keep asking.

They're the ones who lead with curiosity instead of pride.
Who treat learning as a playground, not a performance.

So if fear has been holding you back, try softening it with a little play.

Make the question lighter.
Make it weird.
Make it yours.

And ask it anyway.

C. The Confidence That Comes From Owning Your Curiosity

Confidence isn't loud.
It's not slick or polished or filled with buzzwords.

Real confidence is quiet.
It's grounded.
It's the calm that comes from knowing who you are—and trusting your desire to grow.

And one of the most underrated ways to build that kind of confidence?

You guessed it: **curiosity.**

Curiosity and confidence aren't opposites—they're partners.

Because when you lead with curiosity, you're saying:

> "I believe in myself enough to ask."

"I don't have to pretend to know everything."
"I'm here to learn, and I'm open to what shows up."

And that is a power move.

Asking Isn't Weak—It's Brave

Somewhere along the way, we picked up this idea that asking questions is a sign of weakness.
That not knowing something means you're unprepared, unqualified, unworthy.

That couldn't be further from the truth.

The people who are actually out there doing big things? They're the ones always asking.

They ask for help.
They ask for clarity.
They ask for insight, feedback, collaboration, and new ways of seeing.

They don't need to pretend they have all the answers because they've learned that the real flex is being willing to search for better ones.

Every time you ask a real question, you're reinforcing a powerful belief:

> I am capable of growth.

And that belief? It compounds.

Curiosity Builds Evidence

Confidence isn't just a feeling.
It's built from evidence—little moments where you show yourself what you're made of.

Every time you ask a question instead of staying silent, you create a data point.

- You spoke up in the meeting.
- You asked your client, "What do you really want from this?"
- You emailed the person you admire and said, "Can I pick your brain for 10 minutes?"

It doesn't matter if the answer was yes, no, or silence.
The win was in the asking.

That's how you build inner evidence.
That's how you stop waiting for confidence to arrive and start creating it.

One question at a time.

From Self-Doubt to Self-Trust

Let's be real—when you first start asking questions boldly, it might feel wobbly.

You might second-guess yourself.
Worry about how you'll sound.
Wonder if you're bothering someone or overstepping.

But here's what happens with repetition:

You start to realize... you're still standing.
You're still growing.
You're getting answers. Opportunities. Conversations. New ways of thinking.

And each time that happens, a shift starts to take place.

You go from:

"What if they think I'm dumb?"

To

"What if this is exactly what they needed to hear?"

You go from:

"Do I even have the right to ask this?"

To

"Of course I do."

That's not ego.
That's self-trust.
And it's built by practicing curiosity over and over again, until it becomes part of how you move through the world.

Try This: Gather Your Curiosity Wins

Quick challenge:

Think back over the past few weeks or months.
What's one time you asked a question that led to something good?

Maybe it was small—asking for a book recommendation that turned into a deep conversation.
Maybe it was big—questioning your career path and realizing it was time for a change.

Write it down.

Then write a second one.

Start building your own "Curiosity Wins" list.

You'll start to see something beautiful: a trail of evidence that you are bold, thoughtful, and powerful.

And that power started not with having the answer... but with having the guts to ask.

Own It

When you own your curiosity, you stop outsourcing your confidence.

You stop waiting for someone to validate your questions.
You start trusting your inner voice—the one that wonders, explores, and wants more.

And when you live from that place?

You show up differently.
You lead differently.
You connect differently.

Not because you're louder.

But because you're rooted.

So go ahead—own it.

Be the person who raises their hand.
Who asks the follow-up question.
Who's not afraid to say, "Tell me more."

That's where real confidence lives.

And it looks damn good on you.

D. Asking Better Questions for Personal Clarity

Clarity doesn't usually show up in a lightning bolt.

It's not something that smacks you in the face mid-coffee like, "Oh, hey, here's your life's purpose."

More often?
It comes in whispers.
And you only hear them when you learn how to ask the right questions.

The ones that cut through the noise.
The ones that make you pause.
The ones that sting a little—in the best way.

Clarity isn't about having all the answers.
It's about asking the questions that reveal what's true for you.

You Can't Get Clear If You Don't Get Curious

We all say we want clarity.

Clarity on what's next.
Clarity in our relationships.
Clarity in our careers, our goals, our identity.

But here's the thing nobody tells you:

> Clarity isn't something you wait for.
> It's something you ask your way into.

If you're feeling stuck, foggy, or uncertain, chances are you're recycling the same old thoughts.
And those thoughts are tied to the same old questions—ones like:

- "What am I doing wrong?"
- "Why can't I figure this out?"
- "What should I be doing with my life?"

But better questions create better clarity.

Questions like:

- "What actually energizes me right now?"
- "What have I been pretending not to know?"
- "What would I choose if I wasn't afraid?"

See the shift?

These aren't questions that create shame.
They create movement.
They invite honesty.
They get you to pause and listen—not to the world, but to
yourself.

The Power of a Personal Audit

I like to think of this like doing a curiosity audit on your own
life.

Not a performance review. Not a shame spiral.

Just a real, grounded check-in:

- Where am I feeling resistance?
- Where am I overcomplicating things?
- What feels heavy, and what feels light?

These aren't just fluffy journal prompts.
They're your internal GPS system recalibrating.

Sometimes you don't need to change your whole life.
You just need to change the question you're asking yourself
about your life.

My Own Clarity Moment

When I sat at that mastermind event, and someone asked,
"What's your highest and best use?"—I didn't have a neat
answer.

But that one question cracked the shell wide open.

It made me realize I'd been spending all my energy trying to fit
into the industry mold.
To be what I thought a "successful mortgage professional"
was supposed to look like.

But when I got curious—really curious—I started hearing a different voice.

A quieter one. A truer one.

It asked things like:

- "What if mortgages could feel human again?"
- "What if I trusted myself to do this differently?"
- "What if I could teach, not just sell?"

Those questions didn't just give me insight.

They gave me permission.
To shift. To simplify. To start fresh.

And that's where PBJ Mortgage was born—from clarity that didn't come from a five-year plan, but from a moment of real, raw, honest self-curiosity.

Try This: Curiosity = Clarity

Grab a notebook. Or open your notes app. Right now.

Choose one area of your life where you feel unclear.

And instead of spiraling with "What am I doing wrong?"—try one of these:

- "What's feeling heavy right now and what's that trying to tell me?"
- "What part of me is ready for something new?"
- "If I could be wildly honest, what do I actually want?"

Let the question breathe.
Don't rush to solve it.
Sometimes just holding the question is enough to start the shift.

Clarity Doesn't Always Come Loud

Sometimes it shows up as a gentle nudge.
Sometimes it's just a word, a picture in your head, a gut feeling that won't leave.

But here's what I know:

> If you keep asking brave questions, clarity will meet you in the asking.

It may not come right away.
But it will come.

And when it does?
You'll know exactly what to do next.

Because clarity doesn't live in someone else's advice.

It lives inside your own questions.

E. Staying Curious When You Don't Feel Ready

Let's be real: Curiosity sounds great when life is flowing.

When you're rested.
When things feel manageable.
When you're not drowning in decision fatigue or spiraling in self-doubt.

But what about when you're not in that place?

What about when your inner world feels like a mess?
When your brain is foggy, your body is tired, and you don't feel motivated or focused or "in the zone" at all?

Those are the exact moments when curiosity can be hardest to access—and when it's the most important.

Curiosity Isn't a Vibe—It's a Practice

One of the biggest myths about curiosity is that it's something you either feel or you don't.

But that's not how it works.

Curiosity isn't a mood. It's a muscle.

And like any muscle, you won't always feel excited to flex it. Especially on the hard days. The anxious days. The "I have nothing left in the tank" days.

But the trick is to meet yourself exactly where you are and ask from that place.

Even a small, quiet question is enough to shift the energy.

You don't need to launch into full self-discovery mode.
You just need to stay open—even a crack.

Because curiosity doesn't require perfection.
It just requires willingness.

What If You Just... Started Where You Are?

When you feel overwhelmed, confused, or shut down, try asking:

- "What am I noticing right now?"
- "What's underneath this feeling?"
- "What's the smallest next step I can take that feels true?"

These are low-bar, high-impact questions.

They don't demand that you fix your entire life.
They simply invite you back into the conversation with yourself.

You don't need to be in the perfect headspace to be curious.

You just need to show up and ask something that keeps the light on inside you.

The Lie: "I'll Get Curious When I Feel Better"

Let's call this out.

That voice that says:

- "I'll ask the big questions when I'm more confident."
- "I'll get curious once things calm down."
- "I'm not ready to look at that yet."

That voice sounds protective, but it's actually keeping you stuck.

Because here's the truth:

> Curiosity is how you start to feel better.
> It's not the reward for being ready—it's the path to readiness.

You don't wait until your house is spotless to light a candle. You light the candle to shift the mood.

Same thing here.

You ask the question—even when you're in the mess—to create space. To create breath. To create movement.

A Time I Didn't Feel Ready (And Asked Anyway)

There was a moment not long before PBJ Mortgage was born where I was feeling completely tapped out.

Burnt. Discouraged.
Like I was putting everything I had into a system that didn't reflect who I really was.

I didn't feel brave.
I didn't feel creative.
I sure as hell didn't feel ready to reinvent anything.

But then, at that mastermind event, someone asked a simple but pointed question:

> "What would it look like to build something that feels like you?"

That cracked me wide open.

Not because I suddenly had a clear vision. I didn't.
But because I realized I hadn't let myself ask that kind of question in a long time.

That one moment of curiosity—at a time when I didn't feel ready at all—changed everything.

Not because I was certain.

But because I was willing.

Try This: The Two-Minute Curiosity Reset

Feeling stuck? Try this:

1. Set a timer for two minutes.
2. Ask: "What feels off right now?" or "What do I need in this moment?"
3. Free-write or voice-note your response—no filter, no fixing.

It doesn't have to be profound. It just has to be honest.

And that small act of tuning in can create a shift.

Because the second you start listening, you start leading.

You Don't Have to Feel Ready

You just have to be curious enough to begin.

Curious enough to say,

> "I don't know what this is yet... but I'm willing to look."
> "I'm willing to ask the question, even if the answer takes time."
> "I'm willing to show up for myself—even on the off days."

That's what this work is about.

Not perfection.
Not polished clarity.

Just the courage to stay curious.

Especially when you don't feel ready.

Because that's where your next breakthrough is waiting.

CHAPTER III

From Curious Child to Cautious Adult

"Direct them to what amuses their minds, so that you may be better able to discover with accuracy the peculiar bent of the genius of each."
— **Plato**

A. Remembering Who You Were Before the World Told You Otherwise

Before life got complicated.
Before you learned how to shrink, edit, and filter yourself...
You were wildly curious.

Not calculated.
Not strategic.
Just curious—in the purest, most unfiltered way.

You didn't need a reason to ask questions.
You didn't worry about how your voice sounded or whether your thoughts were "useful."

You were in it for the wonder.

For the delight of discovering something new, the thrill of connecting dots no one else saw, the joy of tugging at a thread just to see where it unraveled.

That wasn't just childhood energy.
That was your essence before the world started layering expectations on top of it.

You Weren't Always This Cautious

Think about it:

No toddler has ever been afraid of looking silly when they ask a question.

They're not second-guessing if they're qualified to ask why the moon changes shape or whether ducks speak the same language as chickens.

They just ask. Boldly. Frequently. Loudly.

Curiosity wasn't something you had to find—it was your default mode.

But then... something shifted.

You learned to read the room.
You learned to play it safe.
You learned to raise your hand a little lower, speak a little softer, and ask fewer "annoying" questions.

Not because you stopped wondering, but because you learned it was safer not to ask.

Maybe it was a teacher who made you feel dumb.
Maybe it was a parent who said, "Don't be dramatic."
Maybe it was a boss who shut down your idea before you finished your sentence.

Little by little, you started trading your natural curiosity for approval.

Not because you're weak.
Because you're human.

And approval, safety, belonging? Those are basic human needs.

So we adapt. We filter. We fold in on ourselves.

But in doing that, we lose access to one of our most powerful tools—our innate, unedited curiosity.

Your Genius Lives in What You Loved Before You Were Told Who to Be

There's a reason that the Plato quote opens this chapter.

He's pointing to something we've known for thousands of years:

> The key to your genius—the thread of your truest self—is in what amuses your mind.

Not what impresses others.
Not what makes the most sense on paper.
Not what keeps you in line.

It's in what lights you up.
What makes you curious.
What you can't not explore.

If you've ever felt stuck or disconnected from your path, this is your cue:

> Go back.
> Revisit the things you loved before someone told you they didn't "make sense."
> Reclaim the questions you used to ask before you were trained to silence them.

Your curiosity hasn't left.
It's just buried under a few layers of "should."

Try This: A Curiosity Flashback

Take five minutes—right now—and think back to when you were 6, 8, 10 years old.

What fascinated you?

- Dinosaurs?
- Space?
- Taking apart the VCR just to see how it worked (and maybe not being able to put it back together)?

What kinds of questions did you ask back then?

Now fast forward to now.

What's the grown-up version of that same curiosity?

- If you loved telling stories, maybe you still crave creative expression.
- If you were always asking how things worked, maybe systems and structure light you up today.
- If you were always the kid helping others figure stuff out, maybe teaching or coaching is in your bones.

This isn't about going backward.
It's about remembering what was already true before life got noisy.

Because the real you?
The curious you?

They've been here the whole time.

You've just been taught to question your curiosity—when the truth is, your curiosity is the question that will bring you back to yourself.

B. How Systems Teach Us to Comply, Not Question

Let's go ahead and name it:

You weren't born cautious.

You were trained to be.

That wild, curious energy you had as a kid? It didn't just fade. It got managed. Redirected. Graded. Corrected.

And over time, you learned the rules of "how things work."

Not just social rules—but systems. Big ones.

School.
Work.
Culture.
Religious institutions.
Family dynamics.
All of it.

These systems—some well-meaning, some deeply flawed— taught you what was "right," "respectful," "appropriate," and "expected."

And more often than not, curiosity didn't make the list.

When the System Rewards the Wrong Thing

Take school, for example.

You're praised for raising your hand only if you know the answer.
You're encouraged to stay on track, follow the rubric, and stick to the prompt.
You're measured not by the quality of your questions, but by the accuracy of your answers.

Even creativity gets boxed in:
Color inside the lines.
Answer the discussion questions correctly.
Write the essay the way they want to read it.

So what do we learn?

Don't ask too many questions.
Don't challenge the material.
Definitely don't push back.

Just learn the system. Play the game. Earn the gold star.

By the time we get to adulthood, most of us are so conditioned to seek approval that we forget how to explore without a map.

The Workplace Isn't Much Better

In corporate life, curiosity is often labeled as disruption.

Ever been in a meeting where someone asked a big-picture question—like, "Why do we do it this way?"—and the energy instantly shifted?

People get defensive. Leaders feel challenged. Colleagues tense up.

It's not because the question was wrong.
It's because the system is built on efficiency, not exploration.

When you challenge "how it's always been done," you're not just being curious—you're rocking the boat.

And a lot of systems would rather stay afloat than move forward.

So again, we learn to zip it.
To keep our heads down.
To just do the job, follow the protocol, and not poke the bear.

Religion, Culture, and "Being Good"

In many families and faith traditions, asking questions is seen as rebellious—or even disrespectful.

Ever been told "because I said so," or "don't question God," or "that's just the way it is"?

That's not just about tradition—it's about control.

Because when people start asking better questions, they start seeing through the cracks in the system.

And people in power? They don't always want the cracks revealed.

But here's what I want you to hear loud and clear:

> You can honor where you come from and question what no longer aligns.
> You can respect your roots and pull weeds when they're choking your growth.

Curiosity doesn't mean you're ungrateful or defiant.
It means you're awake.

Systems Aren't All Bad—But They're Not Sacred

Look, not every system is evil.
Some bring order.
Some create safety.
Some even nurture creativity and growth.

But systems are only as healthy as the values they uphold.

And the moment a system starts punishing questions instead of welcoming them?
That's when you know it's time to reclaim your agency.

Curiosity is how you stay in your power inside the system—or walk away and build something better.

Try This: Rewrite the Rules

Think of a belief or "rule" you were taught growing up.

Maybe it was:

- "Good kids don't talk back."

- "Work comes before everything else."
- "Success means stability, not risk."
- "We don't talk about money."

Now ask:

> "Does this still serve me?"
> "Is this true or just familiar?"
> "What's another possibility?"

You don't have to blow up your life.
But you do get to question the story.

That's how change starts.

Because here's the truth:

You weren't put here to comply.

You were put here to create.
To explore.
To grow into the fullest version of yourself—not the most agreeable one.

And that version of you?
They ask a lot of questions.

Even when the system says not to.

C. Reclaiming the Boldness of Childhood Curiosity

So let's say you've realized it:
You weren't born cautious. You were trained that way.

You see how systems, expectations, and fear slowly layered over your natural instinct to explore.

And now you're wondering...

How do I get that boldness back?

The good news?
It's not lost.
It's dormant.

That fearless, curious, wide-eyed version of you?
They didn't disappear.

They've just been waiting.
For space. For safety. For a little invitation to come out and play again.

This is that invitation.

Think About That Kid You Used to Be

The one who didn't hesitate to raise their hand.
Who took things apart just to see how they worked.
Who asked why five times in a row without a single ounce of shame.

That kid didn't worry about saying the wrong thing.
They weren't editing themselves for professionalism or likability.
They didn't need to be productive to feel valuable.

They were just... curious.
Naturally. Effortlessly. Boldly.

And not because someone told them it was okay.

But because that's who they were.

That's who you are.

Boldness Doesn't Mean Loud—It Means Unapologetic

Let's clear this up:
Reclaiming boldness doesn't mean you have to become one with the loudest voice in the room.

You don't need to throw out your whole life and become a megaphone for change.

This kind of boldness is quieter but more powerful.

It's the boldness of asking the question anyway, even if your voice shakes.
Of challenging the narrative, even when it's uncomfortable.
Of saying, "I don't know, but I want to find out."

It's the boldness of trusting your curiosity more than your fear.

Real Talk: It's Going to Feel Awkward at First

If it's been a while since you let yourself ask the big, brave, maybe-a-little-weird questions... it might feel awkward.

You might stumble.

You might overthink it.
You might have to talk yourself into saying it out loud.

That's okay.

This isn't about nailing it on the first try.
It's about giving yourself permission to try at all.

You're not going backward—you're reconnecting with something true.
Something that was always yours.

The more you practice, the more natural it gets.

And the more natural it gets, the more unstoppable you become.

What This Looks Like in Real Life

Reclaiming your boldness might look like:

- Asking a question in a meeting that no one else is willing to ask.

- Saying, "I'm not sure I agree with that—can we explore it more?"
- Admitting, "I don't know, but I'd love to learn."

It might also look like:

- Following a weird little spark of interest, even if it doesn't "make sense."
- Exploring a new career path or creative outlet just because you're curious.
- Saying, "What if I didn't do it the way everyone else does?"

Boldness doesn't have to be loud.
It just has to be honest.

Try This: A Bold Question to Ask Yourself

Right now, grab your notes app or journal and answer this:

> If I weren't afraid of being wrong, what question would I ask today?

Maybe it's about your work.
Maybe it's about your relationship.
Maybe it's about who you are and who you're becoming.

Whatever it is—don't censor it.

Write it. Sit with it.
Then, if you're feeling bold... ask it out loud.

Your Curiosity is Your Compass

Reclaiming childhood curiosity isn't about being naïve.
It's about being free again.

Free to wonder.
Free to explore.

Free to trust that not knowing doesn't make you weak—it makes you alive.

The world has enough people pretending to have it all figured out.

What we need are more people bold enough to say:

> "I wonder…"
> "What if…"
> "Can we look at this differently?"

And the beautiful thing? You already know how.

Because you've done it before.

Now we're just bringing that part of you back.

A Personal Story: The Question That No One Wanted to Ask

I was always a wild dreamer as a kid.

My mind was a playground. I asked questions that went nowhere—and that was the point. I created big, imaginary worlds. Thought out loud. Wondered boldly. And at first? People loved it. It was cute. It was celebrated.

But over time, the tone changed.

My creativity became "crazy childhood wondering."
My curiosity got labeled "impractical."
Teachers. Parents. Well-meaning adults started telling me, "Be real."

So I learned. I didn't stop being curious—but I did stop sharing it with enthusiasm.

I didn't want to be the weird kid anymore.
I didn't want the eye rolls.
So I quieted it.

Fast forward to adulthood, though—and I'll tell you this: That boldness never fully left me.
I've never been great at following the rules.

Not to be rebellious—but because a lot of rules never made sense to me.
They felt arbitrary. Limiting. Like a lid on something that should've been expanding.

And when I look back, one moment stands out more than any other.

It was my first year of law school—what they call 1L.
I was sitting in Contracts class with Judge Spurlock, a man who could command the room with just a glance. We were deep into a discussion on something called **consideration**—a core concept in contract law.

He kept saying it. Over and over.
And I had no clue what he meant.

In my world, "consideration" meant thinking of someone's feelings.
Like, "Be considerate. Consider others."
But this? This was something else entirely—and I was totally lost.

Now, in law school, especially that first year, the pressure to look like you know what's going on is real. Everyone is trying to sound smart. Everyone is terrified of being the one who doesn't get it.

So the last thing I wanted to do was raise my hand.

But I did.

I raised my hand, heart pounding, fully prepared to look like an idiot.
Judge Spurlock paused, looked at me, and said, "Stand up."

I stood.

I asked:

> "Can you explain what consideration actually means? Because I'm not following."

He let me sit back down.
Then he turned to the rest of the class and asked them my question.

Hands shot up. People had answers.

One by one, they answered—and one by one, he shut them down.

> "No, not quite."
> "Close, but not really."
> "Not the heart of it."

And it hit me.

They didn't know either.
They were all just pretending.

I wasn't the only one with the question.
I was just the only one willing to ask it.

That day taught me something I've carried ever since:

> **Boldness doesn't mean you have all the answers. It means you're not afraid to ask the question.**

That's what childhood curiosity looks like in adult form.
It's not loud or showy.
It's brave.
It's vulnerable.

And it makes space for you and for everyone else who's been waiting for permission to speak up.

CHAPTER IV

Questions as a Tool for Joyful Empowerment

"Don't let anyone narrate your dreams."
— **Akbar Sheikh**

A. Using Questions to Reclaim Your Voice

Let's be real—life has a way of handing you scripts.

Who you should be.
What you should want.
How you should act, dress, parent, lead, and love.

You don't even realize it's happening at first.
But little by little, you start living a story that doesn't fully belong to you.

And here's the thing about stories that don't fit:
They leave you restless. Disconnected.
Like you're succeeding at something that doesn't actually matter to you.

So how do you get your story back?

You ask better questions.

When You Start Asking, You Start Reclaiming

Questions are one of the most powerful tools for reclaiming your voice.

Because when you ask, "What do I actually believe?" or

"What's true for me?"—you stop outsourcing your identity to other people's expectations.

You start filtering the noise through your own values.
You begin writing your own story again.

And that's not just empowering—it's freeing.

Real Empowerment Doesn't Come From Answers—It Comes From Ownership

Here's something we don't talk about enough:

Power isn't about control. It's about choice.

And you can't make aligned choices if you're not asking questions about what you actually want, need, or believe.

Empowerment is about realizing that you get to define success.
You get to reimagine your values.
You get to say, "Actually, that's not for me," without needing to justify it to anyone.

And asking the right questions helps you remember that you're the narrator now.

A PBJ Parallel

This was a big shift for me in building PBJ Mortgage.

There were industry standards, systems, and strategies that were "proven," "professional," and "expected."

But none of them felt human.

So I started asking:

- "What if people actually felt good during this process?"

- "What if we could make mortgages feel simple and approachable?"
- "What if clear communication and personal connection were worth more than jargon and posturing?"

Those weren't just business questions.
They were empowerment questions.

They reminded me I didn't have to follow someone else's model.
I could build my own.
And I did.

Try This: The Power Audit

Let's get practical.

Grab a notebook, journal, or the notes app on your phone.

Choose an area of your life where you feel like you're just going through the motions.
Not failing, necessarily—but not lit up, either.

Ask yourself:

- "Whose voice is running this part of my life?"
- "What would feel powerful, playful, or more like me?"
- "What story do I want to start writing here instead?"

Then just listen.

You don't have to make a big move today.
But even asking these questions opens the door to new clarity and new choices.

Questions Create Joy Because They Create Possibility

This isn't about flipping your life upside down overnight.

It's about waking up to the fact that you have agency.
You get to be curious.
You get to pivot.
You get to dream differently.

And when you ask questions that help you step into your
power, life gets lighter.
More creative.
More joyful.

Not because everything is perfect.
But because you remember: This is your story.

And you don't need anyone else to narrate it for you.

B. Asking Questions That Shift Your Energy and Perspective

Not all questions are created equal.

Some are surface-level.
Some are strategic.
But some—the really good ones—don't just give you answers.
They shift your energy.

They change how you feel in your body.
They reframe your perspective.
They invite in something new.

And that's when curiosity becomes more than a tool.
It becomes a catalyst.

The Question That Changes Everything Isn't Always the Deepest

Sometimes, the question that unlocks something isn't wildly
profound. It's just well-timed.

You could be spinning out in stress, buried in a spiral of "What's wrong with me?" or "Why is everything so hard?"

And then someone—maybe even you—asks something like:

- "What if it's not as complicated as I'm making it?"
- "What would this look like if it were easy?"
- "Is this really a problem, or just a pattern?"

And boom.
Your brain shifts.
Your breath deepens.
You feel your shoulders drop.

That's the power of a question that interrupts the loop and gives your nervous system room to breathe.

Energy Before Strategy

Most people try to solve problems by jumping straight into tactics.

They want the to-do list, the timeline, the ten-step plan.

But if your energy is off—if you're anxious, afraid, overwhelmed—it doesn't matter how "right" the strategy is. You won't follow through. Or you'll self-sabotage. Or you'll build something that looks great on the outside but feels off inside.

That's why I always say: ask the question that shifts your state before you try to shift your situation.

Curious Questions That Create Expansion

Here are a few of my favorite energy-shifting questions:

- "What would feel really good right now?"
- "What am I assuming that might not be true?"

- "Is this mine—or am I carrying someone else's expectation?"
- "How could I make this lighter, easier, or more fun?"
- "What else could be true here?"

These kinds of questions help you zoom out.

They lift you out of tunnel vision and open up possibilities.
They reconnect you with choice.
And in doing so, they move you from a reactive state to a creative one.

A Moment That Shifted My Own Perspective

There was a season where I felt overwhelmed in my business—not because things were failing, but because I was doing too much. Saying yes to everything. Taking on too many clients. Trying to be everything to everyone.

I was exhausted.
And my default was to fix it with more strategy: better systems, more productivity hacks, time blocking, batching—you know the drill.

But then I asked a different question:

> "What would this look like if it were built for joy, not just performance?"

That one line shifted everything.

It gave me permission to redesign—not because things were broken, but because I wanted it to feel better.

More aligned. More human. More me.

That question didn't just change my schedule.
It changed my energy—and that changed everything else.

Try This: Choose One Question to Interrupt the Loop

Think about something you're stuck on right now.
Could be big. Could be small. Doesn't matter.

Now pick one energy-shifting question from this list—or make up your own—and ask it out loud.

Then sit.
Let your mind wander.
See what opens up.

Sometimes the most powerful thing you can do is stop trying to solve the problem—and start asking a better question around it.

Not to fix it.

To reframe it.

Because here's the truth:

> When your energy changes, your choices change.
> When your questions change, your future does too.

You don't need to force clarity.
You don't need to hustle your way into alignment.

You just need to ask the kind of questions that help you see the situation differently.

And once you do that?

Everything else opens up.

C. Asking for What You Want Without Guilt or Shame

Here's something most people won't say out loud:

> A lot of us don't ask for what we want—not because we

don't know what it is, but because we feel like we're not allowed to want it.

We've been trained to be low-maintenance. Easygoing. Grateful for whatever shows up.

And while gratitude is beautiful, it can become a trap when it's used to silence our desires.

"I should be thankful."
"Other people have it worse."
"I don't want to be a burden."
"I'll just figure it out myself."

So instead of asking for what we want, we shrink it.
We delay it.
We bury it under obligations, logistics, or someone else's priorities.

And what happens?

We end up resentful.
Disempowered.
Disconnected from ourselves.

Wanting Isn't Selfish—It's Human

Somewhere along the way, we learned that wanting something makes us needy.
That asking for more makes us ungrateful.
That needing help, support, clarity, space, love, or time means we're too much.

Let's clear that all the way up:

Wanting something isn't a weakness. It's honesty.

And honesty is the foundation of every empowered life.

When you deny what you want, you start living out of alignment.
You make decisions that look good on the outside but feel hollow.
You say yes when you mean no.
You build businesses, relationships, even entire lives around other people's preferences and wonder why it feels like something's missing.

The antidote?
Start asking for what you want.

Out loud.
Without guilt.
Without apology.

But What If They Say No?

Let's talk about the fear under the fear.

Most of us don't avoid asking because we're worried we'll get a "yes."
We avoid asking because we're terrified of the no.

We attach our worth to the outcome.
We think if someone says no, it means our wants were wrong.
Or that we were wrong for asking.

But here's what I've learned—personally and professionally:

> A "no" doesn't diminish your right to want.
> And it doesn't mean the answer is no forever.

Sometimes it just means: not from them.
Not right now.
Not this way.

But at least now you know.

And now you're not stuck in the tension of pretending you don't care.

One of My Own "Ask" Moments

There was a time early in my business when I wanted to shift how I was showing up with clients.

I was doing everything—every email, every meeting, every late-night panic call. And while I loved serving people, I was burned out and starting to resent the very work I used to love.

I remember sitting down and asking myself,

> "What would feel more aligned? What do I really want my role to look like?"

And when I answered honestly?

I realized I wanted more white space.
I wanted to be more strategic, not just reactive.
I wanted to lead—not babysit every detail.

That meant making some changes. Delegating. Setting boundaries. Charging differently. Rewriting expectations.

It felt uncomfortable.
But it also felt right.

Because the more I asked for what I wanted, the more energy I had to serve the people I was meant to serve.

Try This: Name the Want

Right now—without censoring or justifying—ask yourself:

What do I want that I've been afraid to ask for?

It might be:

- A raise.

- More rest.
- More romance.
- A break.
- A chance to start over.
- A straight answer.
- Support.
- Space.

Now write it down.
And then—ask the follow-up:

> "What's the story I've been telling myself about why I can't ask for this?"

This is where the guilt or shame hides. And once you name it? You get to question it.

You get to decide if it's really yours, or if it's just something you inherited.

Asking Is How You Take Ownership of Your Life

You don't have to beg.
You don't have to demand.
You don't have to manipulate or people-please your way into what you need.

You just have to ask.

Clearly. Boldly. Without guilt.

Because you are allowed to want more.
And the first step to receiving more... is being willing to name it and ask for it.

A $1300 Question That Changed a Life

I'll never forget this call I took back in my early days working the phones at the Countrywide call center.

It was a refinance client—someone looking to consolidate debt.
She was in a tough spot financially, and based on the numbers, the refinance made so much sense.

We were going to save her around $1300 a month.

That's not a small change. That's life-changing money.

And yet... she hesitated.

She clearly wanted to say yes. I could feel it. I could hear the longing in her voice. But something was holding her back.

And I didn't want to push—I wanted to understand.
So I asked.

> "I know you want to do this loan, so tell me—what's holding you back? Why aren't you excited to move forward?"

There was this pause. And then she blurted out:

"I can't afford the closing costs."

In that moment, it all clicked.

She didn't know—like so many people don't—that on a refinance, you can roll most of the closing costs back into the loan itself. It's not like a purchase where you need all that cash upfront. She thought she had to come out of pocket for the full amount.

I explained it to her—clearly, calmly, with compassion.

Her relief was instant.

She said yes within minutes. We locked it in.

And she walked away with a loan that literally changed her financial reality.

But here's the part that sticks with me the most:

> If I hadn't asked that question... she would've walked away.
> She would've carried that stress with her.
>
> She would've missed out on $1300 of monthly breathing room—not because the loan didn't work, but because she felt too ashamed to admit what she didn't know.

That moment reminded me how powerful it is to ask—even when it feels risky.
Even when silence would be easier.
Even when it's not "scripted."

Because sometimes the thing standing between someone and what they want most is a single, bold, curious question.

D. Asking the Questions That Lead to Purpose

Sometimes, we ask questions to uncover what others need.
But some of the most powerful shifts come when we ask those same kinds of questions inward.

Because let's be real—most of us aren't walking around totally clear on our purpose.
We're figuring it out one messy step at a time.

But here's the truth that no one talks about enough:

> **Purpose isn't something you find. It's something you uncover through curiosity.**

It's not sitting on a mountaintop waiting for you.
It's hiding in your patterns. In your pull. In your pain.
It's in the moments that make you light up and the ones that make you say, "Something about this matters."

And the only way to get to it?

You've gotta ask.

The Wrong Question: "What's My Purpose?"

Let's be honest—"What's my purpose?" is kind of a terrible question.

Not because it's wrong to want purpose.
But because the way we ask it often triggers more pressure than clarity.

It feels like there's a right answer we're supposed to find.
Like our purpose is some golden key we either have or we don't.

That kind of question puts us in panic mode.
It's too big. Too vague. Too heavy.

So let's shift it.

Let's ask questions that help us notice what's already trying to surface.

Better Questions That Bring Purpose Into Focus

If you want to uncover your purpose, start asking:

- What kind of work makes me forget to check my phone?
- What am I curious about even when no one's watching?
- What kind of problems do I feel emotionally pulled to solve?
- What do people naturally come to me for over and over again?
- What frustrates me—not just annoys me—but makes me want to do something?

These are the questions that don't just show you what you're good at.
They show you what you care about.

Because purpose isn't just about talent.
It's about resonance.

It's that intersection where what you do well meets what you deeply value.

You Don't Need a 10-Year Plan—You Need a Pulse Check

One of the biggest myths about purpose is that it's some long, linear career plan.

Nope.

Sometimes your purpose changes.
Sometimes it evolves.
Sometimes it shows up as a nudge instead of a roadmap.

And that's okay.

Asking questions like:

> "What feels purposeful right now?"
> "Where do I feel pulled, even if it doesn't make perfect sense yet?"
> "What's one thing I could do that would feel more meaningful today?"

...can be enough to get you back into motion.

Purpose doesn't need to be heavy.
It needs to be honest.

My Own Question That Brought Purpose Into Focus

I didn't always know I'd end up here.

Coaching, teaching, helping people get unstuck with money and mindset and mortgage—it wasn't some clear, tidy plan.

It came from curiosity.
From asking:

> "What if I built something that made people feel safe asking questions?"

> "What if the loan process could be simple, empowering—even joyful?"

> "What if I could make the most overwhelming financial decision of someone's life... feel like a PBJ sandwich?"

Those questions weren't business strategy.
They were purpose in action.

And every time I leaned into them, I found more alignment, more clarity, more energy.

Not because I figured out my purpose, but because I followed it.

Try This: Your Curiosity + Your Calling

Take five quiet minutes.
No pressure. No perfection.

Ask yourself:

- What do I feel pulled toward right now, even if it doesn't make sense yet?
- If I could build something that helped others in a way that felt natural to me, what would it be?
- What's one thing I can't stop thinking about—even if I'm afraid to pursue it?

Don't edit the answers.

Let your curiosity take the lead.

Because here's the truth:

> You don't find your purpose in the noise.
> You find it in the questions you dare to ask yourself in the quiet.

And those questions?
They're already inside you.

Let's ask them together.

CHAPTER V

Don't Let Others Dim Your Light

"If you want to fly, you have to give up the things that weigh you down."
— **Toni Morrison**

A. The Subtle (and Not-So-Subtle) Ways People Shut Down Your Curiosity

Let's be real—curiosity can make other people uncomfortable.

Especially when it challenges assumptions.
When it doesn't follow the script.
When it dares to ask, "Is this really the only way?"

You start to speak up.
You start to grow.
You start asking better, bolder, more honest questions...

And suddenly, people start shifting in their seats.

"Who Do You Think You Are?"

Maybe it's subtle—like a passive-aggressive comment or a raised eyebrow.
Maybe it's louder—a colleague talking over you, a friend downplaying your idea, a family member telling you to "be realistic."

They won't always say it directly.
But the message lands anyway:

"Don't make us uncomfortable."

"Don't grow too fast."
"Don't question what we've accepted."

It's not always malicious.
Sometimes it's projection.
Sometimes it's fear.
Sometimes it's people seeing in you something they haven't yet claimed for themselves.

But if you're not careful, you start to internalize it.

The Inner Narrator is Trained by The Outer Voices

If you hear enough versions of "that's not how we do it," or "you're overthinking," or "don't rock the boat," your internal monologue starts to echo those lines.

You go from asking:

"What else is possible?"

To

"Maybe I'm asking too much."

You go from:

"What do I need?"

To

"What will make everyone else comfortable?"

That's how the dimming starts.
Not with a flick of the switch but with a slow turn of the dial.

But here's the truth:

You don't owe anyone your smallness.

You weren't given your curiosity, your insight, your voice just to keep it quiet enough not to ruffle feathers.

Your growth might make someone else uncomfortable.
That doesn't mean you're doing it wrong.

It means you're moving.

And people who are standing still don't always like movement.

Personal Flashback: When I Started Building My Own Way

When I first started stepping out of the traditional mold of the mortgage world, people didn't always get it.

I wanted to talk to clients like people, not transactions.
I wanted to teach, not just sell.
I wanted to make the process so simple that people would say, "That was actually fun."

That didn't fit the script.

People in the industry told me I was being too playful.
Too creative.
Too different.

But here's what I realized:

> I would rather be misunderstood for standing in my truth than praised for fitting into someone else's box.

Because when you build from your truth—even when people don't get it—you attract the ones who do.

The ones who are also looking for a better way.
The ones who want to be lit up.

And those are the people you're meant to serve, support, or build alongside.

Try This: The Dimming Detector

Take a moment and ask yourself:

> Where in my life am I shrinking to keep the peace?
> Whose approval am I afraid of losing if I keep growing?
> Where do I feel myself hesitating—not because I'm unsure, but because I'm worried about how it will land?

Write it down. Be honest.

Then ask the most important follow-up question:

> What would I do if I weren't afraid of being "too much"?

That's your light.

Protect it.
Fan it.
Let it lead.

Rewriting the Rules—Even When It's Uncomfortable

I've always been someone who wanted to live life by my own rules.

It's been the running joke in my family.
While my brother was off trying to bend the rules, I was trying to rewrite them altogether.

And when I started shifting deeper into the financial space—trying to help people, especially women, break free from shame and step fully into their financial power—I hit resistance.

Not just from strangers.
But from someone who loves me deeply.

My mom.

We were in her house at the time—because full transparency?
My own financial house was a mess. I was in rebuilding mode.
Figuring things out. Starting fresh.

And she said, lovingly but clearly:

> "I know you really want to help people… but I just don't
> think they want help. Most people would rather stay
> where they are."

And I got it. I really did.
Because yeah—some people do choose comfort over growth.
Some people don't want to be stretched.
Some people aren't ready to ask the hard questions yet.

But I also knew something else to be true:

> There's a rising wave of people who are ready.
> People who are waking up.
> People who are tired of being quiet, small, stuck, or
> broke—financially or emotionally.
> People who are hungry for a new way.

And I knew in my bones: I'm here for them.

Even if others don't see the vision yet.
Even if people I love question the timing, or the direction, or
the logic.

Even if I'm still walking through the fire of the lesson myself.

Because that's how change works.
You rewrite the rules not when it's easy, but when it's
necessary.

You lead even when your voice shakes.
You show up especially when your situation isn't perfect.
You march to the beat of your own drum—even when you're
borrowing your mama's guest room.

That season wasn't shameful.
It was catalytic.

It reminded me that the exact thing I was being called to do—
to step into my own power, define my own financial success,
and guide others to do the same—was something I had to live
first, not just teach.

And I'll keep doing it.
Even when the resistance is loud.
Even when it's coming from people who mean well.

Because letting other people dim your light doesn't make them
more comfortable.
It just makes you disappear.

And I'm not here to disappear.

B. Letting Go of Needing Permission

We spend so much of our lives waiting.

Waiting for someone to say, "Yes, you're ready."
Waiting for the green light. The invite. The approval.
Waiting to be chosen.

And most of the time?

We don't even realize we're doing it.

Because permission-seeking can wear a lot of disguises:

- "What do you think I should do?"
- "Do you think it's okay if I...?"
- "Will they be mad if I say no?"
- "Maybe I need one more certification, class, podcast
  episode, mentor, spreadsheet, plan..."

Sound familiar?

It's the mental dance of trying to justify your truth through someone else's lens.

Nobody's Coming to Validate You

Here's the uncomfortable truth:
The person you're waiting on?
They're probably not coming.

Not because they don't care.
But because your vision wasn't meant to be clear to them.

It was meant to be clear to you.

Your permission slip doesn't need a co-signer.

You don't need anyone to declare you "ready" before you start asking the big questions or making bold moves.

Your curiosity is enough.
Your insight is enough.
Your inner knowing is enough.

Permission is a Habit—And You Can Break It

So how do you stop asking for permission?

You stop apologizing for what you already know.
You stop over-explaining your ideas.
You stop performing for approval that was never yours to chase.

You start honoring your instincts.

You listen to your gut when it says,

"Hey... I think we're meant for more than this."

And then you move, even if your voice shakes.

The goal isn't to be reckless.
The goal is to be so rooted in your own truth that you don't need someone else to hold the flashlight anymore.

A Permission Moment From My Own Life

I've had so many moments where I caught myself holding back, waiting for someone to say, "Yes, that's a great idea." Or, "Yes, people will take you seriously if you do it that way."

And one that sticks out?

When I first started branding PBJ Mortgage the way I wanted to—not just as a mortgage company, but as a place where people felt empowered, educated, and like they could actually enjoy the process.

I wanted to talk about money in real terms.
I wanted to make it playful. Human. Relatable.
I wanted to strip the fear out of it.

And the voice in my head said, "You can't do that unless you're already wildly successful. You can't lead with ease until you've 'earned' it."

But then I realized—I wasn't waiting on proof.
I was waiting for permission.

Permission to be myself in a space that doesn't always make room for that.

So I gave it to myself.

I built it the way I believed it should be.
I taught the way I wanted to be taught.
I showed up before the "traditionalists" were ready—and guess what?

The right people showed up too.

The people who wanted clarity over jargon.
The ones who were tired of feeling talked down to.
The ones who didn't want to play the game—they wanted to change it.

And all of that began the moment I stopped waiting.

Try This: Write Your Own Permission Slip

Right now, finish this sentence:

> "I no longer need permission to…"

Go big. Be bold. Don't edit.

Maybe it's:

- …change careers.
- …start over.
- …charge more.
- …say no.
- …take up space.
- …ask for what I want.
- …shine.

Then ask yourself:

> What would I do differently this week if I truly believed I didn't need anyone else's approval?

Now go do it. Even if it's one small step.

Because here's what I want you to remember:

> Nobody gets to grant you access to your own light.

It's not a role you audition for.
It's a space you claim.

And once you stop waiting for permission?

That's when everything shifts.

Reader Reflection: The Permission You've Been Waiting For

Take a breath.

Get quiet for a second.
Not Instagram-quiet. Not email-quiet. Soul-quiet.

And ask yourself:

> **Where in my life have I been waiting for permission?**

To pivot?
To ask for more?
To take up space?
To say, "Actually, that doesn't work for me anymore"?

Write it down.

Now ask:

> **Who taught me I needed permission in the first place?**
> **And do I still want them writing the rules for my life?**

You don't have to move a mountain today.
You just have to move yourself. One inch closer to your truth.

So here's your moment:

> **Write yourself a permission slip.**

> "Today, I give myself permission to

> ____
> ____."

Let it be messy. Let it be bold. Let it be yours.

And then?

Read it out loud.
Say it with your chest.
Say it like it's already true—because it is.

C. Turning Down the Noise and Turning Up Your Inner Voice

There's a moment—after you've stopped asking for permission, after you've faced the resistance, after you've decided to stay lit up no matter what—where a new challenge creeps in.

Not from other people.
Not even from old beliefs.

But from the noise.

The constant, low-level hum of opinions, advice, comparison, and pressure that surrounds us every day.

Podcasts telling you how to optimize your morning.
Experts telling you you're doing it wrong.
Family members offering unsolicited advice on your goals, your finances, your timeline.

It's everywhere.

And if you're not intentional, it'll drown out the most important voice of all:

> Your own.

External Noise Is Loud. Your Inner Voice Is Quiet.

Your inner voice?
It's not shouty. It's not pushy.

It doesn't scream over your to-do list or force itself into the conversation.

It whispers.

It shows up in the quiet in-between moments—the pause before you say yes, the tug in your gut when something feels off, the flicker of "what if?" when you're about to play it safe.

But if your life is full of noise—notifications, expectations, obligations—it gets hard to hear it.

And if you don't hear it?

You stop trusting it.

That's when you start crowd-sourcing your direction.
That's when you second-guess everything.
That's when you lose your anchor.

Your Inner Voice Isn't Woo—It's Wisdom

Let's clear this up:

> Listening to yourself isn't indulgent. It's responsible.

Your inner voice isn't reckless.
It's not anti-logic.
It's not a distraction from your goals—it's your most honest source of alignment.

It's the voice that knows when you're saying yes out of fear instead of desire.
It's the one that knows when you're shrinking, settling, or staying small just to make other people more comfortable.

When you start asking questions like:

- "Does this feel like me?"
- "What do I think about this?"

- "If no one else had an opinion, what would I choose?"

…you're tuning in. You're turning the dial down on the outside world and turning it up on what actually matters.

A Personal Check-In I Come Back To

There was a moment when I was building PBJ Mortgage— things were going well, but I could feel myself starting to drift into performance mode.

I was looking around too much.
Paying attention to how other people in the space were branding, speaking, and selling.
And I caught myself thinking: "Maybe I should sound more like that. Maybe I should tone this down. Maybe I'm doing too much."

That's when I paused and asked:

> "Is this idea coming from inside me… or is it coming from the noise?"

That one question snapped me back into alignment.

Because I don't want to be the best version of someone else. I want to be fully me—clear, grounded, curious, and real.

And that means listening to my own voice.
Even when it's quiet.
Especially then.

Try This: The Volume Check

Take a moment to sit still—just for two minutes.

Ask yourself:

- What feels loud in my life right now?

- Whose voice am I hearing more than my own?
- Where do I need to turn the volume down?

Then ask:

> What is my inner voice trying to tell me that I've been ignoring?

Don't rush it. Let it rise.

That voice is still there.
It's been speaking all along.

You're just learning how to trust it again.

Because here's the truth:

> The answers aren't out there.
> They're in here.
> Inside the questions only you can ask yourself—and the voice only you can hear.

And when you get quiet enough to listen?

That's when your life starts sounding like yours again.

Tuning In: A Practice to Hear Your Inner Voice

Let's make this simple.

Find a quiet space. No distractions. Just you.

Set a timer for **five minutes**. (Yes, you have five minutes.)
Grab a notebook, open a voice note, or just sit in stillness.

Now ask:

> "What do I actually want right now?"
> "What am I pretending not to know?"

"What's my inner voice been whispering… that I've been too busy to hear?"

Let the answers rise—without judgment, without filters, without trying to make them perfect.

Let them be messy. Unfinished. Unpolished.
Let them be yours.

Then ask one more:

"What's one small thing I could do today to honor what I just heard?"

Write it. Say it. Feel it. Then do it.

This is the work.
Not the loud, flashy stuff.
The quiet remembering.

Your inner voice is always speaking.

This is how you learn to listen.

CHAPTER VI

Education Through Curiosity

"I have no special talent. I am only passionately curious."
— **Albert Einstein**

A. Why Curiosity Is the Best Teacher You'll Ever Have

We've been taught that education means information.

That learning comes from classrooms, degrees, credentials, and experts with PowerPoint slides.

But the truth?

Your best teacher has always been your curiosity.

It's not just a way of learning—it's a way of living.

Curiosity keeps you asking.

Keeps you growing.

Keeps you alive to possibilities most people walk right past.

And the best part?

You don't have to wait for a syllabus to start.

You Were Learning Before You Were Ever "Taught"

Before school, before grades, before someone told you to "focus"—you were already learning.

You learned through exploration.

Through trial and error.

Through play, failure, and asking a million questions in a row.

That was education.

Raw. Alive. Yours.

But then… the system stepped in.

And education became something to endure.

A box to check.

A series of hoops to jump through in the right order, at the right time, with the right people nodding their heads.

You started learning to pass a test, not to understand.

To please, not to pursue.

And that's when curiosity got pushed to the back row.

But Curiosity Has a Way of Fighting Its Way Back

Because let's be honest—most of the life-changing things you've learned?

They didn't come from a textbook.

They came from a moment when you got curious.

When you asked a better question.

When you were willing to not know.

When you Googled something at midnight or followed a rabbit trail of ideas until it made sense to you.

Curiosity doesn't care if it's "useful."

It just wants to explore.

And when you trust that urge? You start learning everything differently.

I've Learned the Most by Daring to Ask

When I stepped more deeply into the world of personal finance and mindset, there were a thousand things I didn't know.

But instead of panicking, I let myself get curious.

I read, listened, watched, asked—not because I had to, but because I wanted to. Because I was hungry for clarity. Because I wanted to help people feel what I never felt: empowered, educated, and excited about money.

And that learning stuck—not because it was on a test, but because it was tied to purpose.

When you connect learning to meaning, curiosity becomes fuel.

And it burns way longer than motivation ever could.

Try This: Reclaim Your Curiosity as a Learning Tool

Pick one area of your life where you feel behind, stuck, or overwhelmed.

Now ask:

"What am I curious about here?"

- Not "What should I know?"
- Not "What does everyone else already understand that I don't?"
- Just: "What am I genuinely curious about?"

Then follow that.

- Look up a term you've heard but never understood.
- Watch a YouTube video that breaks it down like you're five.
- Ask a friend, mentor, or even AI (hey 🤚) to walk you through it.

Let curiosity be your teacher.

Let learning be led by wonder, not worry.

Because here's the truth:

You don't need more credentials to grow.

You need more curiosity.

And once you trust that?

The whole world becomes your classroom again.

A Life of Learning Fueled by Curiosity

I've been coaching and managing people for the better part of two decades.

But long before that, I was a tutor.

A teacher.

A kid who devoured books like they were oxygen.

I've always been serious about education—not just the kind that hangs on your wall, but the kind that sticks to your bones.

Yes, I hold a bachelor's degree.

Yes, I earned a law degree.

But those credentials are only part of the story.

Because I've never stopped learning.

And I never plan to.

Not because I need more accolades.

But because curiosity won't let me stop.

It's in everything I do—from how I lead, to how I parent, to how I build a business, to how I coach someone through the scariest financial decision of their life.

And here's what I've learned through it all:

The most transformative learning comes not from being told—but from being curious enough to ask.

When people feel safe to wonder—without shame, without judgment—they expand.

When they dig in and ask the question they've been too embarrassed to say out loud, something unlocks.

I've seen it happen in coaching sessions, on sales calls, around kitchen tables, even in myself.

Breakthroughs—real ones—don't always come from experts or strategy decks.

They come from someone being curious enough, brave enough, to ask:

> "What if there's another way?"

That's education at its best.

Not performance. Not perfection.

Just the powerful, joyful act of asking.

Your idea—Creating a Personal Curriculum of Curiosity and Fun—is perfect. It shifts the reader from inspiration to implementation, and gives them permission to explore without tying everything to productivity or performance.

Let's run with that.

B. Creating a Personal Curriculum of Curiosity and Fun

Now that you've reconnected with curiosity as a teacher, and you've let go of needing to perform your way through learning... Here comes the fun part.

You get to build your own curriculum.

No grades.

No deadlines.

No one is breathing down your neck with a red pen.

Just a wide-open invitation to follow your fascination.

Because the point of curiosity isn't to turn everything into a job.

It's to stay alive inside yourself.

To make space for joy, creativity, and new connections.

What Is a Personal Curriculum?

Think of it like this:

If your life had a class schedule based entirely on what lights you up—what would be on it?

What are you hungry to understand, even if it has nothing to do with your career or your five-year plan?

Your personal curriculum isn't about being useful.

It's about being you-ful.

It's a mix of:

- Things you've always wanted to learn but never gave yourself time to
- Questions that keep resurfacing
- Topics that spark a smile when you hear them
- Subjects that make you feel alive, even if you're a total beginner

Build It Like You'd Build a Playlist

Don't overthink it.

You don't need a 10-week syllabus or an Excel spreadsheet (unless that sounds fun to you, in which case—have at it).

Just open your notes app and start a list:

"Things I'm Curious About."

Then add to it as things come up—conversations, books, random questions that hit you while driving.

Here's what might end up on that list:

- How your nervous system actually works
- The history of money
- Attachment styles
- Creative writing
- How to make killer sourdough
- Why people stay stuck
- What joy actually looks like in adulthood
- How your favorite song was produced
- Why you always feel lit up after coaching someone

This isn't homework.

It's heart-work.

And the more you feed this part of yourself, the more whole you feel.

Curiosity Expands You in Ways You Can't Predict

What starts as "just a fun interest" often becomes the key to deeper alignment.

You start following your curiosity down one path, and suddenly it opens a door to something else:

A business idea.

A healing moment.

A new connection.

A shift in how you see yourself.

You weren't looking for a breakthrough—but your brain got playful, and the breakthrough found you.

That's the magic.

Try This: Schedule Curiosity

Seriously.

Choose one hour this week and call it "Curiosity Hour."

During that time, you're not allowed to be productive.

You're just allowed to:

- Learn something that has no ROI
- Ask questions that don't need answers
- Explore something just because it's interesting

It can be a podcast. A documentary. A Google spiral. A journal session. A call with someone who lights up your brain.

No pressure. Just wonder.

Because here's the truth:

Curiosity isn't just for fixing what's broken.

It's for expanding what's beautiful.

And when do you make space for that?

Life gets a little lighter.

A little brighter.

A little more you.

Reflection: Your Personal Learning Playlist

Take a few minutes—grab a notebook, your journal, or the notes app on your phone.

Ask yourself:

> "What have I always wanted to learn, just for me?"

> "What topics, ideas, or questions light me up—even if they don't 'make sense'?"

> "If I didn't need to be productive or impressive, what would I be wildly curious about?"

Now make your list.

Call it whatever you want:

- Your Personal Curriculum
- Curiosity Playlist
- Things That Make Me Feel More Me

Start with five.

Add to it over time.

And most importantly—pick one to follow this week, just because you can.

You're allowed to learn for the joy of it.

No permission slip needed.

CHAPTER VII

Overcoming the Voices in Your Head

"You've been criticizing yourself for years, and it hasn't worked. Try approving yourself and see what happens."
— **Louise Hay**

A. Naming the Voice of Self-Doubt

Let's be real: The biggest blocks to our growth don't usually come from other people.

They come from inside our own heads.

That voice that whispers:

- "Who do you think you are?"
- "You're too late."
- "You're not smart enough to ask that."
- "If you try this and fail, everyone will know you're a fraud."

We all have it. That inner critic or inner doubter—whatever name you give it, it shows up whenever you start stepping into something new, bold, or unfamiliar.

And it's loudest when you're onto something good.

Because the moment you start reclaiming your voice, owning your curiosity, and moving toward your purpose?

That voice gets scared.

It Sounds Like Truth, But It's Not

The most dangerous part of self-doubt?

It doesn't sound like self-doubt.

It sounds like logic.

Like reason.

Like "being realistic."

It borrows the tone of your 8th-grade teacher, or your parents, or the boss who didn't believe in you—and it repeats their words in your own voice.

It tells you to "play it safe."

To "stay small a little longer."

To "be grateful for what you already have."

But here's what you need to know:

> That voice is not your truth. It's your fear—dressed up in familiar language.

And naming it? That's the first step to disarming it.

Why It Shows Up

Your inner critic isn't out to ruin your life—it's trying to protect you.

It's your brain's way of saying, "Hey, remember the last time you got vulnerable and it didn't go well?"

It's trying to keep you safe.

To shield you from embarrassment, rejection, or failure.

But safe doesn't mean aligned.

It doesn't mean empowered.

And it definitely doesn't mean alive.

So when that voice shows up, you don't need to silence it—you need to see it.

You need to say:

> "Ah. I hear you. You're afraid. But I'm growing now. And I've got this."

Try This: Give It a Name

One of the simplest (and weirdly most effective) ways to disarm your inner critic?

Name it.

Not metaphorically—literally.

Give it a name that separates it from you.

Maybe it's:

- Nervous Nancy
- Doubtful Dave
- The Committee
- That One High School Teacher
- Corporate Cheryl
- My Brain Gremlin

When you name it, you stop confusing it with truth.

You start seeing it as a part of you—not the whole story.

So when it pipes up next time, you can smile and say:

> "Thank you, [insert name], but we're not doing that today."

You Can Hear the Voice and Keep Moving

Overcoming the voices in your head doesn't mean they disappear forever.

It means they lose their power to stop you.

It means you get to hear the fear and keep going anyway.

You still get to ask.

You still get to grow.

You still get to show up boldly, curiously, fully—because you're no longer confusing your inner critic with your inner compass.

When the Loudest Voice Was My Own

If you've read this far, it probably won't surprise you to hear this:

> I'm a deeply introspective person.

I live in my head.

I think, analyze, pick things apart, and circle back again—sometimes more times than I'd like to admit.

Pair that with my ADHD and a tendency to hyper-fixate, and you've got a recipe for some serious internal chaos.

And when that inner critic shows up?

She doesn't just whisper—she shouts.

Not enough.

Too much.

They're not going to get it.

This is going to flop.

Why are you even trying?

I've stifled my own growth, curiosity, and momentum more times than I care to count.

Not because of someone else—but because of me. My own voice. My own fear. My own inner pressure.

And honestly? Sometimes curiosity makes it worse before it makes it better.

Because when that inner critic is loud, questioning can get dark.

The "Why not me?" turns into "Maybe it really shouldn't be me."

The "What's next?" becomes "What if I ruin everything?"

But here's what I've learned through experience, not theory:

> You can train that voice. You can interrupt it. You can question it.

One of the biggest lessons came during one of my biggest personal and professional pivots.

I was shifting my business. Starting something brand new.

On paper, it looked exciting—but internally?

I was doubting myself like crazy.

Coaches I admired were questioning my direction.

I was second-guessing every decision.

My inner critic was in full-blown panic mode.

And the only way I made it through?

I turned inward and started asking questions.

"Why am I doing this?"

"What's the real purpose here?"

"Does this feel aligned with who I am—even if no one else gets it yet?"

Not magical affirmations. Not hype.

Just honest, grounding questions.

And you know what?

It didn't erase the voice overnight. But it softened it.

It made space for clarity to rise above the fear.

That experience taught me something I come back to over and over:

> When the critic gets loud, curiosity can speak louder—if you let it.

Try This: Interrupt the Inner Critic

Your inner critic thrives in the dark.

It loves when you keep its script running on autopilot.

So here's how to turn the lights on:

1. Spot the Script

What's the line your inner critic always throws at you?

"You're too late."

"This has already been done."

"You're not qualified."

"If you mess this up, it'll ruin everything."

Write yours down. Own it. Say, "Okay, I see you."

2. Ask a Better Question

Now interrupt it with a curious, compassionate question:

> "Is that actually true?"

> "What if this isn't a sign I'm failing—but growing?"

> "Who says I have to do it perfectly to do it well?"

> "Would I say this to someone I love?"

Questions don't have to be loud to be powerful. They just have to be honest.

3. Create a Comeback

Write one sentence you can come back to anytime the critic shows up.

Something like:

> "I've done hard things before. I'll do this, too."

> "I don't need permission to grow."

> "This voice is fear. And I know how to lead through fear."

Save it on your phone. Stick it on a Post-it. Make it your lock screen if you have to.

This is how you interrupt the spiral.

Not with perfection but with practice.

Now let's keep that momentum moving into the next section...

B. Rewriting the Script with Compassionate Curiosity

Once you name the inner critic and interrupt its usual script, something powerful happens:

You make space for yourself again.

Not the filtered version. Not the performative version.

The real you—the one that's trying to grow, explore, and live in alignment.

But that space only stays open if you fill it with something better.

And that "something better"?

It's not toxic positivity. It's not blind affirmation.

> It's compassionate curiosity.

It's asking, "What's going on underneath this reaction?"

It's meeting your fear with understanding, not judgment.

It's saying, "I hear you… and we're still going."

Your inner critic isn't just annoying.

It's convincing.

It sounds like you.

It knows your fears, your patterns, your insecurities.

It knows exactly what to say to get you to shrink back or stay stuck.

But here's the thing:

> That voice doesn't go away by force. It quiets down with compassion.

Not coddling. Not excuses.

Compassion.

And the tool that makes compassion possible?

Curiosity.

What If You Didn't Judge the Voice—You Just Got Curious?

Most of us try to silence the inner critic by yelling back at it.

But what if, instead of trying to win the argument, you just… got curious?

"What are you afraid will happen if we try this?"

"Where did I learn this story?"

"Is this actually my belief, or one I inherited?"

"What would I say to a friend who was thinking this?"

These questions don't excuse fear.

They disarm it.

They bring the volume down so you can hear what's actually underneath the resistance.

Usually? It's not laziness. It's not a weakness.

It's just fear trying to protect something tender.

Curiosity Creates a Path Forward

Compassionate curiosity doesn't mean you stay stuck in fear.

It means you acknowledge it—and then keep moving.

You say:

> "I hear you. I get why you're scared. But I'm choosing growth anyway."

You remind yourself:

> "There's a reason I'm being pulled toward this—even if I don't feel 100% ready."

And you ask:

> "What's the smallest next step I can take with courage today?"

That's what rewriting the script looks like.

Not perfection.

Practice.

Not confidence.

Curiosity.

A Note About Grace

Let's be clear: Curiosity isn't always easy.

Some days, you'll forget to ask the questions.

You'll believe the fear.

You'll sit in the spiral longer than you meant to.

That doesn't mean you're failing.

It means you're human.

And being human means you get to try again—every single time.

Every moment is another chance to choose a kinder story.

Even this one.

Try This: Flip the Script

Choose one inner-critic phrase you've caught yourself thinking recently.

Example:

> "I always mess this up."

"No one takes me seriously."

"If I speak up, I'll look stupid."

Now, rewrite it—not with fluff, but with curiosity and compassion.

"What can I learn from this pattern?"

"What would it look like to trust my own voice here?"

"What would I say if my child or best friend were thinking this?"

Keep it honest. Keep it gentle.

Let that become your new script.

And read it back to yourself anytime the old one shows up.

Because here's the truth:

You don't overcome self-doubt with force.

You outgrow it with curiosity, compassion, and practice.

And every time you choose that—every time you meet fear with softness instead of shame, every time you ask why instead of what's wrong with me—you rewrite the story.

One question at a time.

One pause at a time.

One gentle comeback at a time.

That's how you become someone who doesn't just silence the critic, but leads anyway.

Not because the fear is gone.

But because the truth is louder.

C. The Origin Story of the Inner Critic

Before your inner critic ever had words... It had a job.

It wasn't born to sabotage you.

It wasn't trying to make you feel small or stuck.

It was trying to keep you safe.

And the way it learned to do that?

By observing your world and building rules to help you survive in it.

Your Inner Critic Is a Protector in Disguise

The part of you that now says:

> "Don't speak up, you'll sound dumb."

> "You always mess things up when you try something new."

> "Who do you think you are?"

...may have first emerged when you were a child trying to make sense of a moment that felt scary, embarrassing, or disappointing.

- Maybe you answered a question in class and got laughed at.
- Maybe you failed at something you cared about and didn't feel supported.
- Maybe you were told to be quiet, to stop being "so much," to stay in line.

So your brain did what it's built to do:

It protected you by creating internal rules.

"Don't take that risk again."

"Don't speak until you're sure."

"Don't want too much."

And those rules?

They worked for a while.

They kept you out of harm. They helped you get praise. They let you belong.

But now?

They've become outdated strategies trying to run a life that's evolving.

You're no longer the person who needed them to survive.

You're the person who's ready to grow.

The Critic Uses Your Past to Control Your Future

The inner critic's logic is this:

> "Last time you tried this, you got hurt. So don't do it again."

It's not just protecting your reputation; it's protecting your nervous system from anything that even resembles past pain.

But here's the catch:

When you don't question those inherited rules, your critic starts to run the show.

And suddenly, you're living a life that reflects your fears, not your desires.

So... Where Did Yours Come From?

Your inner critic may be echoing:

- A parent who held you to impossible standards
- A teacher who dismissed your questions
- A coach who only valued performance
- A community that made you feel like your worth was tied to success or image or control

That doesn't mean those people were bad.

It just means they were human. And so are you.

Naming where those voices come from isn't about blame.

It's about awareness.

Because once you see it, you can choose differently.

Try This: Trace the Voice

Pick one of your go-to inner critic thoughts.

Maybe it's:

"I'm not good with money."

"People like me don't get to have big dreams."

"If I slow down, I'll fall behind."

Now ask:

- Where did I first learn this?
- Who modeled this belief for me?
- What was happening in my life when this voice got loud?

Then ask the follow-up:

> Is this belief still serving me? Or is it a strategy I've outgrown?

This is how you break the cycle.

Not by fighting the voice.

But by understanding it.

Because here's the truth:

> You can love the part of you that learned to protect you and let it know—gently, clearly—it's not in charge anymore.

That's what healing looks like.

That's what rewriting your inner script begins with.

When "Too Much" Becomes a Rule You Carry

I've always had a big personality.

Big voice.

Big energy.

Big ideas.

Big questions.

My mom used to tell people that when I was a newborn—one week old, barely here—I stayed awake from 9am to 9pm without a nap. Just wide-eyed and alert, taking everything in. She said I didn't want to miss a thing.

And that was me.

Curious. Expressive. Always going.

Even before I could talk, I was already asking questions with my eyes.

But here's what else I remember:

Being told to lower my voice.

To tone it down.

To sit still.

To stop moving. Stop talking. Stop questioning everything all the time.

Not always in a mean way.

But enough that the message stuck:

> "You're too much."

Too loud.

Too emotional.

Too opinionated.

Too passionate.

And when you hear that message enough—especially from people you love or trust—it gets in your bones.

In high school, I had friends who told me they loved me, but I was "a lot."

Too intense. Too deep. Too everything.

So I did what so many of us do.

I turned inward.

Maybe that's where my introspection really started.

Not as a conscious, beautiful practice—but as a kind of survival.

Because if I couldn't be small on the outside... Maybe I could be quieter on the inside.

I started shrinking. Questioning myself.

And not the good kind of questioning.

Not the expansive, curious kind.

The painful, looping kind.

> "Why am I like this?"

> "Why can't I just be easier?"

> "Why can't I tone it down?"

And those questions became the critic.

They became the filter I started running everything through.

Even the best parts of me.

D. A New Way to Speak to Yourself

If reading this chapter stirred something in you—good.

That means you're paying attention.

That means you're becoming aware of how the voice in your head was shaped, how it speaks, and how you no longer have to obey it.

Because here's the truth:

> You are not "too much."

You were never too much.

You were just in rooms that couldn't hold all of you yet.

But now you're learning to hold yourself.

To stop shrinking.

To stop editing.

To stop running your worth through other people's filters.

And this is where we begin to speak differently—to ourselves.

Try This: Your Voice, Rewritten

Take a moment. Close your eyes. Take a deep breath.

Ask yourself:

> What is one belief I've carried about myself that I'm ready to release?

(Too loud. Too emotional. Not smart enough. Never ready. Whatever it is—name it.)

Write it down.

Then write a new belief to stand in its place—not a fluffy affirmation, but a truth you're ready to try on:

> "I'm allowed to take up space."

> "My voice is worth hearing."

> "Curiosity isn't a weakness—it's a gift."

> "I can be both growing and worthy at the same time."

Now speak it out loud.

Say it like you mean it, even if your voice shakes.

Say it like it's already true, even if you're still learning to believe it.

Because this is how the critic gets quieter.

Not when you finally "earn" your enoughness...

...but when you choose to stop questioning it.

You've done a lot of work already.

You've questioned the world around you.

You've questioned your own voice.

You've softened the critic, cracked open the rules, and made space for truth to rise.

And now—something shifts.

You're not just reclaiming your own voice anymore.

You're learning how to create space for other voices, too.

Because when you learn to be curious with yourself?

You start listening to others differently.

You stop scanning for what's wrong.

You start seeking what's real.

You stop performing connections.

You start creating it.

This next chapter isn't about small talk.

It's not about impressing, fixing, or proving anything.

It's about presence.

It's about connection.

It's about remembering how powerful it is to genuinely care.

CHAPTER VIII

Being Interested in Others—The Secret Sauce to Deep Connection

---

"Being heard is so close to being loved that for the average person, they are almost indistinguishable."
— **David Augsburger**

A. Why Being Curious About Others Changes Everything

Let's start with a little truth bomb:

Most people don't feel truly seen.

They're used to conversations that skim the surface.

They're used to nodding while someone waits for their turn to speak.

They're used to performance—everyone playing the part, no one actually asking the real questions.

But when you show up with genuine interest?

Something sacred happens.

Walls come down.

Minds open.

Hearts soften.

Your curiosity becomes a gift. Not just for you—but for the person in front of you.

Let's be honest—most people are used to being seen on the surface.

We live in a world full of quick scrolls, half-listens, and "uh-huh" responses while someone's eyes dart toward a screen.

But here's the truth:

> The deepest form of connection isn't about saying the right thing.

It's about making someone feel seen.

And the fastest way to do that?

Genuine, honest curiosity.

Not because you're trying to get something.

Not because you want to impress them.

But because you actually care.

People Can Feel the Difference

You know it. You've felt it.

There's a difference between being asked,

> "So, what do you do?"

...and someone asking,

> "What made you want to do that?"

One scratches the surface.

The other cracks something open.

Because when someone is truly interested—not just in your role, but in your reason—you feel it in your body.

Your guard lowers. Your brain relaxes.

You stop performing and start sharing.

That's what curiosity does.

It builds bridges in seconds that would take years with small talk.

Being Curious Isn't a Trick—It's a Superpower

You don't need a coaching certification, a therapist's license, or a stack of books on emotional intelligence to connect deeply with people.

You just need to show up curious.

To ask:

- "What's something you're thinking about lately that no one's asked you about?"
- "What do you wish people knew about you that they don't?"
- "What's bringing you joy right now?"

These aren't complicated questions.

But they change the energy of a conversation instantly.

Because they do something that most people rarely experience:

They signal, "I'm here for who you are, not just what you do."

Why This Matters More Than Ever

In a world full of people talking over each other, broadcasting instead of listening, and optimizing every moment for attention...

Genuine curiosity is radical.

It slows things down.

It makes room.

It creates safety—and that safety opens doors to truth, vulnerability, and even healing.

And the wildest part?

> You don't need hours to connect. You just need intention.

A three-minute question can feel deeper than a 30-minute conversation if it's asked with presence.

Try This: Practice Micro-Curiosity

Next time you're in a conversation—even a casual one—try a little curiosity experiment:

When someone shares something (even something small), follow it up with:

> "Tell me more about that."

> "What was that like for you?"

> "How did that feel?"

You don't have to force it.

You don't have to sound profound.

You just have to be present.

Not ahead of them. Not analyzing them.

Just with them.

This is how trust is built—one moment of curiosity at a time.

It's not about asking perfect questions.

It's about asking with presence.

And when you start showing up like that?

You'll notice something beautiful:

> People soften around you.

They open up.

And they start asking better questions, too.

Because curiosity isn't just contagious.

It's connecting.

B. The Science of Feeling Seen

When someone says, "I just felt really seen,"—it's not just emotional language.

It's biological.

Real curiosity changes the brain.

It shifts brain chemistry.

It creates physiological safety.

And it builds emotional trust faster than almost anything else.

That feeling we get when someone is genuinely interested in us?

That's not just "nice."

That's your brain and body entering a state of connection—one that's built into your wiring.

Curiosity and the Brain: A Dopamine Supercharger

When you show real interest in someone, it sparks curiosity in them too.

And that curiosity triggers a release of dopamine—the brain's "reward" chemical.

- Dopamine isn't just about pleasure. It's about motivation and focus.
- When someone feels your curiosity, it activates their own sense of interest, attention, and meaning.

This is why a great conversation doesn't just feel fun—it feels energizing.

You're literally helping someone's brain light up by caring about them.

And get this—studies show that when people feel seen and valued, they retain more information, feel less stress, and build stronger relational memory.

Mirror Neurons: Why Curiosity Creates Emotional Safety

You've heard the phrase "Empathy is contagious," right?

That's not a metaphor—it's mirror neurons.

These are specialized cells in the brain that activate both when we do something and when we see someone else doing it.

So when you lean in, ask thoughtful questions, and show nonjudgmental interest?

Their brain mirrors that energy back.

Their nervous system relaxes.

Their guard drops.

They feel safer—and more connected—because your curiosity signals:

> "You're safe here. You matter. You're allowed to take up space."

The Reticular Activating System: What You Focus On Expands

Let's talk about your RAS—the Reticular Activating System.

It's your brain's internal filter, constantly scanning the world and deciding what to pay attention to.

When you're genuinely curious about someone, your RAS says:

"Hey, this is important. Pay closer attention here."

You start noticing the tone. Emotion. Subtext.

You start asking better follow-up questions.

And the person you're with feels that.

They feel like they matter—not because you're "trying," but because your brain is actually tuned in to them.

This is how we build emotional intelligence—not from scripts, but from attention.

Curiosity Calms the Nervous System

You've probably felt this yourself:

You're in a vulnerable moment... and someone listens—not to fix, not to rush—but to understand.

What happens?

Your breath slows.

Your shoulders drop.

You feel safer.

That's not just emotional—it's physiological regulation.

- When you're met with presence, your cortisol (stress hormone) levels go down.

- Your vagus nerve (which controls relaxation and digestion) activates.
- You enter the ventral vagal state—the social, safe zone of your nervous system.

That's the zone where connection happens.

Where growth happens.

Where trust lives.

And all of that? Triggered by presence and curiosity.

So Yes—You're Actually Changing Lives

When you're curious about someone—not to fix them, not to lead the conversation, but to understand them—you're doing something rare:

You're giving them a physiological and emotional experience of being safe.

And in a world that constantly tells people to perform, prove, or polish themselves to be worthy of attention?

Your curiosity becomes a kind of medicine.

It doesn't just make you better at relationships.

It makes the people around you feel more human.

Try This: Ask the Brain-Soothing Questions

Next time you're in a real conversation, try asking:

- "What's been sitting on your heart lately?"
- "What's something that feels heavy—or surprisingly light?"
- "What do you wish people asked you about more often?"

These questions don't just connect minds.

They connect nervous systems.

C. The Curious Connector: How to Ask the Questions That Create Real Bonding

Being a curious connector isn't about being the most interesting person in the room.

It's about being the most interested.

People remember how you made them feel.

They remember the questions that made them pause.

They remember the way your eyes didn't dart away, the way your presence said, "You don't need to shrink here."

This is what makes curiosity a superpower in relationships, leadership, parenting, and even business.

Not forced intimacy.

Just honest, grounded, generous attention.

The Energy Behind the Question Matters More Than the Question Itself

You don't have to ask some perfectly worded, vulnerable-shaking soul-melter every time you talk to someone.

Sometimes the most powerful connection is in how you ask:

- Are you rushing?
- Are you trying to sound deep?
- Are you asking to fix—or to truly understand?

The energy of curiosity is calm, open, and invitational.

It's:

> "Tell me more, I'm here."

Not:

> "Tell me more, so I can prove something."

That subtle shift changes everything.

Go Beyond "How Are You?"—Without Being Weird About It

Let's be real: We've all been on the receiving end of someone trying too hard to ask "a powerful question."

But curiosity isn't about digging for someone's trauma.

It's about creating space for someone's truth—whatever that truth is in the moment.

So instead of:

> "How are you?"

Try:

- "What's something that's been giving you energy lately?"
- "What's been surprisingly hard this week?"
- "What are you looking forward to—even if it's tiny?"
- "What's been on your mind more than usual?"

The goal isn't to get a specific answer.

It's to show someone you're here for whatever's real.

Be Willing to Follow the Thread

One of the biggest mistakes people make in connection?

They ask a question...

... and don't follow the thread.

They get a surface-level answer—

> "I've just been busy lately."

> "Things are good, just a lot going on."

And instead of a curious follow-up, they move on.

But the magic lives in the follow-up.

In the gentle, honest moment where you say:

> "Busy with good things or heavy things?"

> "Want to tell me what's been going on?"

> "You said that kinda quickly—do you really mean it, or are you just being polite?"

These don't have to be confrontational.

They just have to be invitational.

They say, "You're allowed to take your time here. I'm not in a rush to get to the next thing."

That's how trust is built.

Connection Isn't Always Deep—But It Can Always Be Real

Not every moment has to be heart-explodingly vulnerable.

Some of the most powerful connections are built through small, consistent curiosity:

- Remembering the thing someone mentioned last week.
- Sending the book you talked about.

- Following up on how their meeting went.
- Noticing when their energy shifts—and gently asking why.

Real connection is less about one big, deep conversation.

And more about showing up with presence, over and over.

That's what makes people feel safe.

That's what makes them open up.

That's what makes your presence magnetic.

Try This: The Curious Connector Framework

Here's a simple three-part structure to help you practice being a curious connector:

1. Start with the moment.

> "What's been on your mind this week?"

> "What's something you've been thinking about more than usual?"

2. Follow the thread.

> "That sounds like it matters to you—tell me more."

> "How did that feel?"

> "What's underneath that?"

3. Reflect back.

> "That makes sense."

> "I can totally see why you'd feel that way."

> "Thanks for sharing that—most people wouldn't say it out loud."

This isn't a script. It's a rhythm.

And when you start living in that rhythm?

You don't just connect better—you become the kind of person people feel safe around.

That's the real win.

The Call That Changed Everything

If you've read this far, you've probably figured this out about me:

> Curiosity isn't just something I value—it's something I live.

But the real secret?

My greatest strength has always been curiosity about others.

I don't mean nosiness.

I mean genuine, heartfelt interest in what makes people them.

Their stories. Their patterns. Their spark. Their fears.

And learning how to ask the right questions—especially the ones that make people feel safe to tell the truth?

It's changed everything in my life.

I've worked in mortgage for over 20 years.

It's a wildly intimate process—people have to financially bare themselves in ways they often don't even do with family.

And from the very beginning, I found that when I led with curiosity, when I asked just one more thoughtful question and really listened, walls dropped.

I can't tell you the number of times people told me,

"I've never shared this with anyone before."

And I wasn't having these conversations in cozy living rooms or one-on-one video chats.

I was in a call center.

A loud, high-pressure, numbers-driven environment where connection shouldn't have mattered.

But it did.

In fact, it mattered so much that my conversion rates were consistently 25% higher than the average loan officer—and I did it with fewer calls.

Not because I had some slick script.

Because I was curious.

Because I cared.

Because I asked questions that helped people feel seen.

One of the moments that stuck with me the most?

A call with a man refinancing his home.

It started like any other, until he shared—just in passing—that his wife was pregnant.

And I lit up. We celebrated. We talked about names and cravings and all the beautiful unknowns of new parenthood.

I figured we might stay in touch long enough to discover the baby's gender before the loan closed.

But I was wrong.

This was right after the housing crash. The merger between Countrywide and Bank of America was in full swing. And everything was delayed. Everything.

The average loan closed in 30–60 days.

Theirs?

Seven months.

And they stayed.

They waited.

They held on.

Because we had built something.

A relationship.

A trust.

A thread of connection rooted in nothing more than a shared hour and a few real questions.

That baby was born before their loan closed.

And while I wished they'd gone somewhere that could have served them faster, I'll never forget what they taught me:

> When you make someone feel seen, heard, and held— even for a moment—it changes everything.

It creates loyalty.

It creates understanding.

It creates something sacred in the most unexpected places.

So no—this chapter isn't about small talk.

It's about transformation.

Because genuine curiosity about others?

It will win you trust, deepen every relationship you have, and become the secret sauce to a rich, connected, and unbelievably fulfilling life.

And the best part?

It doesn't take much.

Just one question.

One moment.

One open heart.

Reflection Prompt: The Question That Connects

Think of someone in your life—friend, client, partner, colleague—who might be carrying something just beneath the surface.

Now ask yourself:

> "What's one question I could ask them this week that would help them feel seen?"

Not a fixer.

Not a performance.

Just a moment of presence.

Write the question.

Then ask it.

Then listen.

Because one small question might be the thing they remember for years.

CHAPTER IX

Staying the Path—Persistent and Playful Curiosity

"Curiosity is not a luxury; it's a discipline."
— **Elizabeth Gilbert**

"Nothing in this world can take the place of persistence. Talent will not: nothing is more common than unsuccessful men with talent. Genius will not; unrewarded genius is almost a proverb. Education will not: the world is full of educated derelicts. Persistence and determination alone are omnipotent."
— **Calvin Coolidge**

A. Curiosity as a Long Game

Most people think curiosity is a burst of inspiration.

A lightbulb moment.

Something you chase when life feels exciting or when you have the energy for it.

And that's exactly why most people stop being curious.

Because curiosity—real, lasting curiosity—isn't just for when life is easy.

Curiosity is not a spark. It's a path. And staying on that path takes practice.

Curiosity Gets Harder When Life Gets Loud

You won't always feel curious.

There will be seasons where your inner world is quiet, and seasons where your to-do list is louder than your questions.

- The kids need a hundred things.
- Your inbox is overflowing.
- You've got big deadlines, heavy emotions, zero space to think.
- You're burnt out or bored or somewhere in between.

And in those seasons, curiosity can feel like a luxury you can't afford.

But here's what I want you to hear:

> Curiosity isn't something you do when you're already inspired.

It's something you reach for to find your inspiration again.

It's Easy to Be Curious When You're Lit Up

Of course, it's easy to ask questions when life feels expansive.

When you're in a room that excites you.

When your brain is buzzing.

When the world feels wide open, and you're thinking, "What's next?"

But what about when the spark's gone dim?

What about when everything feels like a repeat of a repeat?

What about when you've asked the questions and feel like you still don't have the answers?

That's when curiosity becomes a choice.

That's when it becomes a discipline.

Discipline Doesn't Mean Rigid. It Means Devoted.

People don't love the word "discipline."

It sounds cold. Strict. Heavy.

But that's not what I mean here.

Discipline is just a devotion to returning.

Returning to your practice, your power, your questions—even when it's not convenient.

It's the quiet decision to ask:

> "What's here that I haven't seen yet?"

> "What might be possible even in this stuckness?"

> "What am I pretending not to know?"

Even small questions like these can snap you out of autopilot and drop you back into presence.

Curiosity is a Kind of Resilience

This is why curiosity is more than emotional fluff.

It's mental strength. It's heart fuel. It's strategic survival.

Because when everything else feels stale or hard or uninspiring, curiosity is what helps you:

Reframe instead of retreat

Stay open instead of shutting down

See meaning in the middle of monotony

Ask better questions when your old answers stop working

And the people who stay curious the longest?

They're not the ones with the easiest lives.

They're the ones who've learned how to find wonder even in the waiting.

Try This: A Question to Keep You on the Path

When you feel yourself disconnecting—tired, numb, reactive, or just checked out—pause and ask:

"If I were curious right now, what would I ask?"

You don't have to feel it yet.

Just ask from the intention of curiosity.

What am I noticing?

What might be underneath this feeling?

What's here that I haven't welcomed yet?

Let that question be your anchor.

Because curiosity isn't just what makes life exciting.

> It's what makes life yours.

And when you commit to returning to it—not just when it's easy or sexy or fun, but when it's uncomfortable, inconvenient, or quiet—that's when it becomes powerful.

That's when it moves from an idea... to a way of being.

And in that space?

Growth happens.

Ideas resurface.

Alignment deepens.

You're not waiting for lightning to strike anymore.

You're learning how to carry your own spark.

B. Balancing Discipline with Joy

The words discipline and play don't usually show up in the same sentence.

One sounds serious and structured.

The other sounds light and spontaneous.

But here's what I've learned—through experience, failure, reinvention, and the science behind it all:

> You don't stay curious long-term by choosing between discipline and joy.

You stay curious by choosing both.

The Neuroscience of Persistent Curiosity

Let's get nerdy for a minute.

Curiosity feels like a spark—but underneath, it's powered by dopamine—the same brain chemical responsible for motivation and learning.

Here's what happens when you engage with a topic or question that excites you:

- Your brain releases dopamine
- You experience a little "hit" of energy and interest
- That positive feeling reinforces the behavior
- You're more likely to come back to the process again
- Over time, you build new neural pathways (thank you, neuroplasticity!)

But here's the kicker:

> You don't get that dopamine hit every time unless you keep showing up.

So what do you do when the spark feels dim, or the subject gets hard?

You use discipline to return.

And you use joy to stay.

Why Joy Keeps the Flame Alive

Think of joy as rocket fuel for curiosity.

It's the thing that makes even the hard parts of learning feel worth it.

It's what turns a daily practice into a delightful one.

In one study, educators found that curiosity paired with playfulness—especially in childhood—led to stronger long-term memory and higher academic performance . Adults are no different. When we attach positive emotion to learning, growth becomes more sustainable.

But joy doesn't always mean dancing around in glitter.

Sometimes joy is quiet. Subtle. A moment of Oh... that's interesting.

Joy shows up when:

- A question leads somewhere unexpected
- You rediscover wonder in something old
- You feel free to explore without pressure
- You follow a rabbit hole just because you want to

That's not a distraction. That's alignment.

The Practice of Playful Discipline

So how do we put this into practice?

We build a rhythm that makes room for both structure and surprise.

Try this:

- Set a non-negotiable container for curiosity.

Maybe it's 15 minutes every morning where you journal questions or research something you've been wondering about. Not for work. For you.

- Let one day a week be a curiosity sabbath.

Explore something wildly unrelated to your job. Read about whales. Study the psychology of colors. Rewatch a documentary that made you cry the first time.

- Build a "playlist."

Not music—projects. Keep a list of things you'd love to explore "when you have time." Then make time.

These micro-disciplines create space for macro-wonder.

Joy Doesn't Mean Chaos—It Means Curiosity Without Shame

The goal isn't perfection. It's presence.

You don't have to master every new idea.

You just have to be open enough to explore.

And when you can come back to the path over and over again—not because you have to, but because you want to—curiosity becomes something sacred.

Discipline helps you return.

Joy helps you stay.

Together, they make you unstoppable.

When I Almost Walked Away

In 2023, I wanted to quit mortgages.

I was done.

The lack of loyalty? Soul-crushing.

The way people compared me—after two decades of deep expertise—to someone brand new or worse, treated my advice like it held no weight? It drove me up a wall.

I didn't spend 20+ years becoming an expert just to be second-guessed by an Instagram post.

And what made it worse?

The entire way we connected with people was changing.

Gone were the days of long, meaningful conversations.

We were in a TikTok world now—where people expected to already know what I stood for before they ever picked up the phone.

That felt impossible.

That felt personal.

So I stepped back.

Not to burn it all down, but to ask myself—honestly—what now?

"Do I even want to do this anymore?"

That's when discipline and joy showed up.

Not in some shiny, glamorous way.

But in the form of questions.

Hard ones. Repetitive ones. Relentless ones.

> Why did I ever start this work?

> Why mortgage, of all things?

> Why keep showing up in an industry that felt brutal, male-dominated, cutthroat—and wildly unforgiving?

The answers surprised me.

I loved people.

I loved helping them take on something big and scary and complicated—and breaking it down.

I loved watching someone succeed when they thought it wasn't possible.

And I loved that owning a home could be a real wealth-builder, a generational shift.

That clarity—birthed through discipline—was the reset I didn't know I needed.

And then joy started to whisper again.

Not loud. Just enough.

A new idea. A next question.

> What if I started a second business to help people succeed beyond the mortgage?

> What if I launched a podcast?

> What if I wrote a book?

I didn't have the roadmap.

I had a spark.

And I trusted it.

Because I wasn't willing to give up on being curious.

And I was finally willing to chase what felt joyful—not just what felt productive.

Discipline got me to the table.

Joy reminded me why I built it in the first place.

Reflection Prompt: Return to the Spark

Think of a time when you almost gave up—on a goal, a project, a dream, or even yourself.

Now ask yourself:

> What helped you stay?
>
> What part of you kept showing up, even when you were tired or uncertain?
>
> Where did joy or curiosity sneak in and light something up again?

Write it down.

Let it remind you that the spark isn't gone.

It's just waiting to be invited back.

You don't have to feel on fire every day.

You just have to stay close enough to feel the heat.

C. The Power of "Why Not?" and "What If?" in Facing Challenges

If discipline and joy are the foundation of sustained curiosity, then "why not?" and "what if?" are the rocket fuel.

These are the questions that don't just help you endure challenges.

They help you reimagine it.

They shake the dust off your perspective.

They interrupt fear.

They unlock doors that logic said were locked tight.

> "Why not?" is curiosity with a little rebellion.

> "What if?" is curiosity with imagination.

And when the path gets hard, those two are your best companions.

"Why Not?" Breaks the Rules You Didn't Know You Were Following

So many of us live by invisible scripts.

- You have to follow this path to be successful.
- You can't pivot now—you've come too far.
- You can't charge that. You can't try that. You can't be that bold.
- That's not how it's done.

But who said so?

"Why not?" is the question that challenges the rulebook you never agreed to.

- Why not start over at 40?
- Why not go for the job you think you're not "qualified" for?
- Why not build a business that actually feels good?
- Why not charge what it's worth?
- Why not rest and rise?

These questions don't always give you clear answers.

But they create permission.

They widen the frame.

And sometimes?

That's all you need to move forward.

"What If?" Turns Fear into Possibility

Fear loves to ask its own kind of "what if" questions:

- What if this fails?
- What if they judge me?
- What if I lose everything?

That's fear weaponizing imagination.

But you can reclaim that same power.

You can flip the question and create space for hope:

- What if it works?
- What if I'm more ready than I think?
- What if this hard moment is actually leading to something better?
- What if this is where everything starts to shift?
- "What if?" is a bridge from fear to vision.

It's your mind reaching past what's known into what's possible.

These Questions Don't Just Shift Your Mindset—They Shift Momentum

One honest "What if?" can unblock a stuck moment.

One rebellious "Why not?" can rewire an entire career path.

They're not just fluffy affirmations.

They are disruptors—pattern breakers that let you move forward when everything feels tight.

And the best part?

You don't need to be brave all the time.

You just need to be curious enough to ask the question.

Try This: Build a "Why Not/What If" List

Pick an area of your life where you feel boxed in right now—work, money, relationships, creativity, energy.

Now write:

- Three things you wish you could do but feel off-limits
- Three fears that have kept you from doing them
- Then rewrite each one with a "Why not?" or "What if?"

Example:

- I wish I could take a sabbatical.
- I'm afraid it'll ruin my momentum.
- What if it actually gives me the clarity I need to grow faster when I come back?

Let those questions breathe.

Let them pull you forward.

Because your next breakthrough might not come from pushing harder.

> It might come from asking one bold question you haven't dared to ask yet.

The Questions That Changed Everything

For a long time, I didn't trust myself.

I had spent years learning to quiet my voice, second-guess my instincts, and outsource my power. I was ambitious, yes—but I was also uncertain. Always scanning for external validation before I made a move.

And if I'm honest?

I struggled to find my why.

It wasn't that I didn't care—I cared deeply.

But I didn't always know where that care was leading me.

Then something shifted.

I started playing with two simple questions:

> "What if...?" and "Why not?"

I wrote them down. I said them out loud. I let them disrupt my thinking. I let them lead.

- What if I could run a business differently—my way?
- Why not pitch myself to that publication?
- What if I stopped waiting for someone to invite me to the table and built my own?

And slowly, things started to change.

I was asked to write for major publications.

I made connections I had once only dreamed of.

I stopped shrinking. I stepped into my power. And once I did?

I wrote an entire book in four months.

While holding down two jobs.

While producing my own podcast.

While co-hosting two more.

Not because I had more time or energy than anyone else.

Because I finally stopped waiting for the perfect plan—and started asking better questions.

This stuff works.

It really is that simple.

I get it—"Ask questions." Sounds light. Sounds obvious.

But if you put in the reps?

If you do the work?

If you stay consistent with your curiosity?

It will change everything.

It will become your superpower.

It will unlock the version of you that's been waiting to rise.

And the only thing standing between that version of you and the one reading this page?

One question you haven't dared to ask—yet.

Reflection Challenge: Ask the Braver Question

Find a quiet moment.

Open your journal, your notes app, or even the back of a napkin.

And ask yourself:

What's one bold "What if?" I've been afraid to speak out loud?

What's one "Why not?" that I've been brushing aside—because it feels too big, too soon, or too out there?

Now write it. Don't filter it.

Then ask:

- What's the very next question I could ask to move toward it?
- What's one small step I could take this week to follow the thread?

You don't have to have all the answers.

You just have to be curious enough to keep asking.

Because you don't stay on the path by knowing where it ends.

You stay on the path by daring to wonder what else might be possible.

CHAPTER X

Stretching Your Limits Through Inquiry

"Logic will get you from A to B. Imagination will take you everywhere."
— **Albert Einstein**

A. Using Imaginative Questions to Identify and Push Boundaries

Here's the quiet truth most people don't realize:

You're already living inside boundaries.

The question is—who set them?

Some were inherited.

Some were imposed.

Some you unknowingly drew yourself, out of fear, habit, or a need to stay safe.

But if you want to grow, to stretch, to tap into the real edge of your potential?

You have to start asking:

"What's on the other side of this line?"

And that starts with imagination.

It starts with the questions that don't begin in logic—but in wonder.

Curiosity Isn't Just for Clarity—It's for Expansion

Most people use curiosity to figure something out.

- How do I fix this?
- Why did this happen?
- What should I do next?

That's useful. It's necessary. But it's also limited.

Because the deepest growth, the boldest ideas, and the biggest breakthroughs?

They don't come from asking what's known.

They come from asking what's possible.

- What if I let myself want something bigger?
- What if there's another way to do this—one that hasn't been invented yet?
- What if I'm not stuck—I'm just standing at the edge of the next level?

These are the questions that don't always have answers—but they unlock expansion anyway.

The Brain Science of Imaginative Questioning

Imaginative questions activate what neuroscientists call divergent thinking—the ability to generate creative ideas by exploring many possible solutions.

This process lights up the default mode network of the brain— the same area active during daydreaming, storytelling, and visioning.

Here's what that means practically:

- Your brain starts to build connections between unrelated ideas.

- It becomes more comfortable with ambiguity.
- You increase mental flexibility (which is directly tied to innovation and adaptability).

So when you ask a question that feels "too big" or "too out there," you're not being ridiculous.

You're giving your brain permission to play—and that's where creativity lives.

Imaginative Curiosity Pushes the Edges Without Forcing the Outcome

The best part about these questions?

They don't require immediate action.

They don't need to make sense right away.

They just need to be asked.

"What if I built the thing I can't stop thinking about?"

"What if I'm meant for something I haven't even imagined yet?"

"Why not try it my way, just to see what happens?"

These questions stretch your limits without shame.

They don't say, "You're not enough."

They say, "You're not done yet."

Try This: Map the Edge of Your Current Limits

Grab a sheet of paper or your notes app.

Draw a quick mental map:

- In the center: something you're currently working on, dreaming about, or stuck in.

- Around it: List the "rules" you've internalized about it. (Be honest.)

I have to do it this way.

I can't afford to take that risk.

It has to happen on this timeline.

People like me don't do that.

Now ask:

> "What if none of those were true?"

> "What would I try if I let go of those rules for just one day?"

> "Where could I go from here if I stopped thinking in straight lines?"

Let your imagination stretch. Let your questions expand.

Because this is where transformation begins.

Not at the finish line.

At the edge of what you think is possible.

The Peanut Butter and Jelly "What If"

When I created PBJ Mortgage, I wasn't trying to be clever.

I was asking a real question:

> "Does this have to be so serious?"

Yes—mortgages are a big deal.

Yes—it's one of the most important transactions of someone's life.

Yes—there are legal documents, financial disclosures, and 10,000 acronyms.

But that didn't mean the experience had to feel cold, corporate, or soul-sucking.

I was sitting in a mastermind event, thinking about branding.

Not just logos and color palettes—but identity.

> How did I want people to feel when they thought of us?

> What did I want the experience of working with our team to be like?

And then it hit me: PBJ.

Simple. Wholesome. Playful.

Something everyone knows.

Something no one expects in the mortgage world.

It had that sticky, nostalgic factor (pun absolutely intended).

But more importantly?

It gave people permission to breathe. To relax. To trust.

We're the "boring" part of the homebuying process, sure.

But what if we made it feel like the most delightful part? Or at least not the least delightful part!

That one whimsical "What if?" turned into a brand, a movement, a message.

It broke the mold—because I was willing to ask a question that sounded silly at first... and trust that the answer could be brilliant.

B. The Role of Playful Questioning in Innovation and Creativity

Here's the irony about adulting:

We spend our childhoods asking questions like "Why is the sky blue?" and "What if dogs could talk?"

Then we grow up… and stop asking anything that doesn't have a spreadsheet or a "return on investment."

But here's the thing:

> Playfulness is not immaturity.

> It's mental flexibility.

> It's cognitive agility.

> It's the birthplace of creative genius.

And the people who learn how to ask curious, playful questions as adults?

They don't just survive—they innovate.

Playfulness Unlocks New Possibilities

Research shows that when we approach a problem with a sense of play, our brains activate divergent thinking—the exact mode we need for creativity and innovation .

Playful questioning doesn't mean we don't care.

It means we're not locked into one solution.

It means we're asking:

- What if this didn't have to be so complicated?
- What would this look like if it were fun?

- What's the weirdest, wildest idea I can come up with?
- If there were no rules, what would I try?

These kinds of questions let your brain breathe.

They invite possibility where pressure used to live.

The Best Ideas Often Start with Laughter

Einstein didn't sit in a boardroom with a 10-step plan when he developed theories that reshaped science.

He was known for playing with ideas—daydreaming, scribbling, and asking strange questions that didn't always have clear answers.

And some of the world's best inventions?

They started with questions that sounded ridiculous.

- "What if you could carry 1,000 songs in your pocket?"
- "What if people wanted to sleep in a stranger's house?"
- "What if you could hail a taxi from your phone?"

Playful. Weird. Wild.

And world-changing.

You Don't Need a Brainstorm Session—You Need a Brain Break

If you're feeling stuck, burned out, or creatively dry, the answer isn't to try harder.

It's to ask softer.

Take the pressure off. Get weird. Get curious.

- Ask the dumb question.
- Try the idea you'd normally laugh at.

- Put something upside down just to see what happens.

Playfulness opens the creative valve.

It's where joy meets intelligence.

It's what makes work worth doing again.

Try This: The Playground Question Challenge

Set a 10-minute timer.

Choose a challenge you're facing—big or small.

Then ask yourself five playful questions about it.

Make them wild. Make them weird.

Don't try to "solve"—just explore.

Here's a starter list:

- What if this were a scavenger hunt?
- What if I had to make this fun for a seven-year-old?
- What would I do if failure didn't count?
- What if I sang my to-do list?
- What would I try if I had absolutely nothing to lose?

You might laugh.

You might cringe.

But don't be surprised if an idea sneaks in... that actually works.

C. Embracing the Unknown Through Curious and Fun Exploration

Here's something we don't talk about enough:

> You don't have to have it all figured out to take a step forward.

Most people think they need more information, more certainty, more strategy before they can try something new.

But curiosity?

It doesn't need a five-year plan.

Curiosity says, "Let's just see what happens."

Curiosity says, "I don't know where this leads, but I'll go anyway."

That's the power of exploration.

And not just exploration with spreadsheets or post-it notes.

I'm talking about fun.

Unexpected fun.

Slightly-chaotic, light-hearted, rule-breaking wonder.

Because when you let yourself explore without needing a specific outcome, you become free.

Curiosity and Uncertainty Can Coexist

The biggest lie perfectionism tells us is that we have to know before we go.

But think about childhood.

Think about play.

You didn't know what would happen when you built that fort, or tried to jump off the swing set, or made up that wild game.

You didn't care.

You were just in it.

Curiosity made it safe to try.

Imagination made it safe to fail.

You didn't need a guarantee.

You just needed a little wonder.

And guess what? That version of you?

They're still in there.

You just haven't invited them out in a while.

Exploration Isn't About the Outcome—It's About the Expansion

When you explore something with no pressure to produce, you gain something more important than a finished product:

You gain possibilities.

- You test a new idea and feel your confidence grow.
- You say "yes" to something weird, and it leads to someone unforgettable.
- You follow a hunch, and it takes you exactly where you didn't know you needed to go.

This is the essence of creative living.

It's not about betting the farm every time.

It's about being available to surprises.

The Brain Loves Novelty (Even If You're Nervous)

Here's the cool part: Your brain is wired for exploration.

- When you try something new, your brain releases dopamine—reward, pleasure, engagement.
- Even if the thing is small, your nervous system gets a positive jolt.

- This fuels learning, memory, and resilience—which is why new experiences can spark massive personal growth.

But it only works when you're willing to start—even in the unknown.

So the question becomes:

What small, brave, slightly fun thing are you willing to try—even if you don't know what comes next?

Try This: The "I Don't Know, But Let's See" List

Pick one area of your life where you've felt stuck, rigid, or overly cautious.

Now write a list of three to five things you could explore just for the fun of it.

Not because you're supposed to.

Not because they'll give you a guaranteed return.

Just because they feel a little playful. A little strange. A little unknown.

Some ideas:

- Try a creative project in a medium you've never touched.
- Ask someone a wildly open-ended question and see where it leads.
- Go somewhere you've never been to in your own city and talk to someone new.
- Watch a documentary on a topic you know nothing about.

- Say yes to the thing you'd normally hesitate on—and just see what unfolds.

Let curiosity lead.

Let outcomes go.

> Because clarity isn't always found in thinking harder.

> Sometimes, it's found in moving forward—laughing, exploring, and learning as you go.

D. Rediscovering the Fearless, Playful Exploration of Childhood

There's a moment in childhood—before the world teaches us to be careful, quiet, and strategic—where we're wildly unfiltered with our curiosity.

We didn't ask questions to get it right.

We asked because we wanted to know.

We played not to win, but to wonder.

And then, somewhere along the way, we learned:

- To raise our hands only if we were sure
- To laugh a little less loudly
- To color inside the lines
- To stop asking too many questions

We didn't stop being curious.

We just got quieter about it.

But here's the truth:

> That version of you didn't disappear.

They're still in there—just waiting to be invited back out.

Curiosity Is Fearless When It Isn't Measured

Kids don't need a return on investment.

They don't care if their ideas sound ridiculous.

They're not wondering how it'll land on LinkedIn.

They just ask:

- What happens if I mix this and this?
- Can I build it taller?
- Why does the moon follow me when I walk?

That's not childish.

That's wisdom most adults have forgotten.

> Because true curiosity doesn't need credentials.

It just needs permission.

Wonder Isn't Just for Kids—It's Fuel for Grown-Up Growth

You don't outgrow curiosity.

But you can forget how to use it if you never let yourself play anymore.

So maybe it's time to:

- Try something ridiculous.
- Let an idea sound silly for a while.
- Ask a question that makes zero sense... and follow it anyway.
- Take one small risk with no purpose other than joy.

You're not being irresponsible.

You're being alive.

Try This: Reconnect with Little You

Take a deep breath. Close your eyes.

Picture yourself as a kid—five, six, maybe seven years old.

What lit you up?

What were you curious about, obsessed with, constantly imagining?

What did you love to explore—not because someone told you to, but because you couldn't help it?

Now ask:

> How can I bring just a piece of that back into my life this week?

You don't need to go full finger-painting (unless you want to).

But could you ask one question without worrying how it sounds?

Could you explore something just to feel light again?

Let that kid lead for a little while.

They didn't lose their magic.

They've just been waiting for you to remember.

Now's the perfect moment to drop your story. Something that connects you back to your childhood curiosity or a moment in adulthood where you caught a glimpse of it again. Light, whimsical, but honest.

The Christmas I Asked for Books

When I was a kid, I was obsessed with reading.

I mean obsessed.

One Christmas, I asked for only one thing:

> Books. That's it.

> No toys. No games. Just stories.

My mom still talks about that Christmas. She says it was my best one ever—and her most depressing.

She said she felt sad watching me blow through the entire stack of books they bought in less than a week. Those were my only gifts, and I devoured them before the New Year even hit.

But me? I wasn't sad.

I had lived a dozen lives.

Traveled to other worlds.

Stepped into people's hearts, minds, and stories.

All from the comfort of our living room floor.

That's the thing about books.

They make you wildly curious.

They invite you to imagine without limits.

I was so immersed, so connected, so sure that I saw what the characters saw, felt what they felt...

That for at least three or four books into the Harry Potter series, I was convinced Hermione Granger wore glasses.

Why?

Because I wore glasses. And clearly, she must've too.

That's the kind of fearless, playful curiosity we're talking about.

The kind that doesn't ask for permission.

The kind that doesn't worry about getting it wrong.

The kind that makes the world bigger just by asking, "What if…?"

It's not gone.

It's just been buried under grown-up expectations, timelines, and responsibilities.

But here's the good news:

You don't have to go back to childhood.

You just have to invite that part of you forward.

Ask a silly question.

Get lost in a story.

Let your imagination stretch into places your logic forgot existed.

Let that little kid lead for a while.

They knew exactly what they were doing.

Reflection Prompt: Let the Wonder Back In

Think back to something you were wildly curious about as a kid.

What did you love exploring just because it lit you up?

What made you lose track of time?

What felt magical, even if it didn't make sense?

Now ask yourself:

> Where can I let a little of that wonder back in—today?

> What would it look like to follow that curiosity... just for fun?

Write it down.

Then try it.

Just a little.

Because grown-up breakthroughs often begin with childlike questions.

CHAPTER XI

The Ripple Effect of Curiosity

"Don't underestimate the power of your presence. Sometimes the most radical thing you can do is simply show up as your whole, curious self—and give others permission to do the same."
— **Unknown**

A. How Your Fun Questions Can Inspire and Energize Others

There's something electric about being around someone who's genuinely curious.

They're not trying to impress you.

They're not rushing to solve your problems.

They're just... there.

Open. Engaged. Playful. Fully present.

And when someone shows up like that?

It gives you permission to show up differently, too.

Your Curiosity Becomes Contagious

We've all felt it:

- That moment someone asks you a question you've never been asked—and it lights you up
- That feeling when someone listens not just to respond, but to understand

- That shift in energy when someone's presence makes you feel safe to be honest, unpolished, real

That's the ripple of curiosity.

And it doesn't require a title or a mic or a platform.

It just takes attention.

And a willingness to care out loud.

Fun Questions Create Brave Spaces

You might not realize it, but your playful questions are often the first domino.

They make it okay for others to:

- Drop the act
- Be honest about what they want
- Admit they don't have it all figured out
- Dream bigger than they've let themselves dream in a long time

Sometimes, the most powerful thing you can do for someone else isn't to give them the right answer.

It's to ask the question that unlocks the right part of them.

Real Influence Doesn't Shout—It Invites

Curiosity isn't pushy.

It's invitational.

And people feel that.

In a world that's full of noise, fast answers, and big opinions, your quiet willingness to ask and wonder and not rush becomes a radical kind of leadership.

Not the loud kind.

The transformative kind.

Try This: Become a Question Catalyst

Think of someone in your world who seems stuck, stressed, or disconnected.

Instead of giving advice or trying to fix it, ask:

> "What's a question no one's asked you that you wish they would?"

Or even:

> "What would feel fun to explore right now—even if it doesn't make sense?"

Let your curiosity hold space for someone else's clarity.

Because that's how the ripple begins.

The Breakup Girl Theory

I have a running joke—one I've told more times than I can count:

> I was always the girl guys dated just before they met "the one."

Seriously. I don't know how many times I've dated someone, and the very next person they dated? Boom. Wife.

It used to bother me. Like, was I the romantic warm-up act? The emotional preseason? The spiritual Costco sample before the full meal?

But over time, I realized why it kept happening.

> It was curiosity.

I've always been curious. You know that by now. And that extended into dating.

When I started dating seriously in college (shoutout to genetics for the late glow-up), I didn't do surface-level small talk. I asked real questions. Not because I was trying to "get serious" right away, but because I've always believed you can't figure out alignment without understanding someone's truth.

So I asked things like:

- What do you actually want out of life?
- What drives you?
- What scares you?
- What lights you up?

And you know what happens when you ask those kinds of questions on dates?

> You get answers. Real ones.

You learn what someone values, what they dream about, what they're avoiding. You go deep.

And when you do that, clarity comes quickly.

Not just for me, but for them.

Most of the guys I dated were wonderful people. Kind, driven, interesting. We just weren't aligned long-term. And because I was paying attention—and asking questions that mattered—I saw that clearly.

So when it came time to end things, I didn't do the cliché "It's not you, it's me."

I did something a little different. I'd say:

> "It's both of us."

I'd explain that we were just misaligned. That we were both great, but moving in different directions. And then I'd do something else:

I validated their desires.

I'd say things like, "What you want really matters. You should go after that. And I hope the next person you meet is someone who gets it and gets you."

And you know what?

That little ripple of curiosity and permission may have helped some of them find that next person.

I don't know for sure, but I have a strong suspicion:

By asking deeper questions, by modeling emotional honesty and playful vulnerability, I helped them see more clearly what they really wanted.

That's the ripple.

It doesn't always look like a TED Talk.

Sometimes it looks like a thoughtful breakup over coffee, or in my case tea.

But make no mistake—curiosity can change someone's life.

Even when they don't realize it right away.

B. Creating a Culture of Joyful Inquiry in Your Environment

Curiosity doesn't just live in questions—it lives in the energy those questions create.

And when you consistently model curious, open-hearted, nonjudgmental inquiry?

You change the room.

You create a culture.

Whether it's your team, your clients, your family, your classroom, or your group chat, people start to sense:

- It's safe to wonder here.
- It's okay not to know here.
- I won't be judged for asking here.
- My thoughts matter here.

And that?

That's where bold ideas are born.

That's where honest conversations start.

That's where people stop performing and start being real.

Your Questions Set the Tone

If you're a leader, a parent, a teacher, a coach—or simply a human who interacts with other humans—your curiosity sets the temperature of the space.

People feel when you're genuinely interested.

They feel when you're just asking out of habit.

And they feel when you're asking to guide, to connect, or to create space for truth.

So ask yourself:

- What kinds of questions am I modeling right now?
- Do they open doors... or shut them?
- Do they invite people in... or push them into defense?
- Do they spark play... or pressure?

Curiosity Builds Trust Faster Than Competence

This is especially important in work environments. You don't have to be the smartest person in the room to lead well.

You just need to create a space where people feel like:

- They can speak without being shut down.
- Their ideas aren't "dumb" just because they're different.
- They can explore without needing to be right immediately.

Competence gets respect.

Curiosity builds trust.

And trust is what makes a culture sustainable.

Joyful Inquiry Is a Practice, Not a Policy

You don't need a team retreat or a whiteboard to build a culture of inquiry.

It starts with everyday interactions.

- Ask your kids, "What's something you're curious about today?"
- Ask your team, "What's one thing we haven't tried because it felt too bold?"
- Ask your friends, "What's been lighting you up lately?"

These aren't radical questions. But they create a radical connection.

Try This: Start the "Question of the Week"

Want to build a curiosity culture without forcing it?

Start a simple rhythm:

> A question of the week.

It could be in your team Slack, your family dinner table, your Instagram stories, or a shared group text.

The rules:

- No judgment
- No "right" answers
- Just one question that invites thought, story, or surprise

Some ideas:

- "What would you try if you didn't have to be good at it?"
- "What part of your week felt more meaningful than you expected?"
- "What do you miss that you didn't realize you'd lost?"

Let people answer in their own way, on their own terms.

The point isn't participation. The point is presence.

Because when people get used to questions like that?

They stop waiting for permission to be curious.

They just become it.

C. The Global Impact of a Playful, Questioning Mindset

Let's zoom out.

We've talked about how curiosity changes your mindset. How it deepens your relationships. How it creates new possibilities in your immediate environment.

But here's what we don't talk about enough:

Curiosity changes the world.

It's not just an individual advantage.

It's a cultural force.

Curiosity Has Powered Every Major Leap Forward

Across history, the greatest revolutions—scientific, technological, social—have all started with someone asking a bold, inconvenient, sometimes dangerous question.

- "What if the Earth isn't the center of the universe?" — Galileo
- "What if we could fly?" — The Wright Brothers
- "Why can't women vote?" — the suffragists
- "What's it like to be in someone else's shoes?" — empathy-based activism

From the Enlightenment to civil rights movements, from moon landings to global storytelling projects like Humans of New York, curiosity has challenged what was "normal" and made space for what could be.

> "Most of the breakthrough discoveries and remarkable inventions throughout history... are the result of curiosity."

Curious Cultures Are More Innovative and Resilient

According to research published in Harvard Business Review, organizations that nurture curiosity at every level—by encouraging questions, rewarding new ideas, and making space for exploration—are more innovative, adaptable, and high-performing. Why?

Because curiosity drives learning, creativity, and collaboration—especially in uncertain times.

And it's not just companies. Entire communities and cities thrive when curiosity is encouraged. Think:

- Science fairs
- Public libraries
- Hack-a-thons
- Interdisciplinary schools and community art centers

These aren't fluff. These are innovation engines.

And When Curiosity Gets Shut Down? Progress Stalls

Conversely, when curiosity is discouraged—whether in classrooms, workplaces, or entire governments—something dangerous happens.

People stop asking.

Ideas go stale.

Injustice festers.

Potential withers.

This is more than theory. It's been documented across history, from authoritarian regimes that punish questions to corporations like Blockbuster and Kodak that ignored internal innovators raising red flags .

> "When curiosity is punished, people stop asking. And that kills innovation at its roots."

Curiosity Crosses Borders and Bridges Divides

One of the most powerful roles curiosity plays is in cross-cultural understanding. It helps us:

- Ask before assuming
- Listen instead of labeling

- Learn before reacting

Projects like Humans of New York became global sensations not because of production value, but because of curiosity and compassion—two forces powerful enough to stir global empathy one photo and story at a time .

Try This: Make Curiosity a Global Act

Ask yourself:

> "What's one belief I hold that I've never truly questioned?"

Then:

> "Whose experience might challenge this belief—and what could I learn from them?"

This isn't about doubt. It's about depth.

Big change doesn't require a podium.

It requires an open mind.

And a willingness to keep asking.

You Drove... In Taiwan?

My curiosity has taken me all over the world.

Literally.

All 50 states. 27 countries. And what I've found is this:

> Curiosity bridges gaps better than anything else I've ever seen.

One of my favorite stories happened in Taiwan.

Of all the places I've traveled, Taiwan was probably the least westernized—which isn't a bad thing at all. But it did highlight just how different things can feel when you're fully outside your linguistic and cultural comfort zone.

Everything was in Mandarin characters. Very little English was spoken.

But my husband and I were curious.

So we rented a car to explore beyond the big city—winding our way into the mountains, just to see. We'd heard those mountains were famous for their tea, and sure enough, we stumbled across a little tea shop perched on the side of the road.

The couple who ran it greeted us with huge smiles and what looked like... mild panic.

The man kept frantically dialing his phone, trying again and again to reach someone.

Meanwhile, the woman simply poured us tea.

We tasted, nodded, and smiled.

She poured more. We nodded again. We liked it. She smiled bigger.

Finally, the man's phone rang. He answered in a flurry, then thrust the phone into my hand.

On the other end was what I can only assume was his son.

He spoke English and started asking all the questions:

- Where are you from?
- Why did you come to Taiwan?
- How did you get to this tea shop?

When I said we drove, he repeated it slowly like he couldn't believe it.

"You drove? In Taiwan?"

I laughed.

Yes. We're Americans. Yes, we rented a car.

Yes, we were curious enough to just figure it out.

And I'll never forget the way his voice shifted—how surprised he was that we wanted to experience his country, not just as tourists, but as people who were genuinely interested in the real lives, real places, and real people of Taiwan.

That curiosity stunned him.

And I like to think it sparked something in return—maybe a little curiosity toward us, too.

Because curiosity is reciprocal.

When you care, others start to care too.

When you wonder about others, it invites them to wonder about you.

We didn't speak the same language.

We didn't have the same culture.

But we had something better:

A mutual willingness to be fascinated.

That's the ripple.

And it's one of my favorite stories ever.

D. Nurturing Curiosity and Play in the Next Generation

Here's something I've learned over and over again:

When you step into your power with curiosity, you give others permission to do the same.

Especially the next generation.

Especially the people closest to you.

> Whether you're a parent, a coach, a leader, a friend, or just someone paying attention—your energy becomes contagious.

Kids Don't Do What You Say—They Mirror What You Model

You can talk all day long about the importance of being curious.

You can encourage your kids, or your team, or your students to "ask big questions" or "use their imagination."

But if you're not modeling that in real life?

- If they never see you try something new…
- If they never hear you say, "I don't know, but let's find out…"
- If they never watch you light up about learning something weird or wonderful…

Then it's just theory.

And theory doesn't change people.

Embodiment does.

What they remember isn't the instruction. It's the invitation.

You Don't Have to Have It All Together

Sometimes the most powerful thing you can model isn't mastery—it's openness.

Let your kids see you:

- Try something you've never done before

- Ask a question you don't already know the answer to
- Read something silly or wildly interesting just because you're curious
- Get excited over a discovery, even if it's small or strange

Let your team watch you:

- Change your mind after asking better questions
- Pause to wonder instead of rushing to fix
- Invite their ideas—not just tolerate them

This is how you build a curiosity culture—not just with words, but with witnessing.

Curiosity Isn't Just Teaching Kids How to Think—It's Teaching Them They Matter

When you ask a child (or a teammate or a partner), "What do you think about that?" or "What are you wondering about?"—you're doing more than sparking learning.

You're signaling that their thoughts have value.

That their perspective counts.

That their voice belongs in the conversation.

This is how self-trust is built.

This is how leadership is shaped—long before it's named.

Try This: Create Micro-Moments of Shared Curiosity

You don't need a whole workshop or a workbook. Start small.

- At dinner, ask "What was something weird or interesting you noticed today?"
- With your team, try "What would make this process feel 10% more fun?"

- With yourself, pause mid-scroll and ask, "What's something I haven't looked at in a while... but want to?"

The moment doesn't have to be big.

It just has to be real.

Because one question—asked with presence, asked with love—can change how someone sees themselves.

Curiosity is legacy work.

Ask boldly. Model joyfully.

And watch what grows.

For Kat

I have the cutest, most wildly curious daughter named Kat.

She's only three, and already—she sees the world with eyes wide open. Everything is interesting. Everything is worth asking about. Everything is an adventure.

And watching her move through life like that?

It reminded me why I started writing this book in the first place.

Because this—this unfiltered, unshakable wonder—is what we all started with.

But not all of us got to keep it.

Kat reminded me of how powerful curiosity is.

But more than that—she reminded me how fragile it can be if we're not careful.

And I realized something important:

It's my job, as her mother, to protect that spark.

To nurture it.

To make sure the world doesn't kill it—but fosters it. Day after day. Year after year.

She doesn't need to be told who to be.

She just needs permission to keep wondering.

And she's always watching.

Lately, I've noticed she's been saying "I can't" more than she ever used to.

She didn't start life with that phrase. It wasn't part of her vocabulary.

So where did it come from?

Probably me. Or someone. Or something.

Because our kids absorb everything—not just what we teach, but how we talk, how we move, how we ask or don't ask, how we respond to the unknown.

That was a wake-up call.

Because if I'm not mindful... Kat could end up just like I did:

- Hiding her power
- Shrinking her questions
- Playing small to avoid standing out
- Silencing her own voice before it even finds its volume

And that?

That's the cost of not protecting curiosity.

So now I ask myself every day:

What would it look like to model wonder—to show her what it means to stay open, to stay brave, to keep asking?

What would it sound like to be the voice of abundance, not limitation?

Because that's what we all need.

Not just as kids, but as grown-ups trying to remember who we were before the world told us who to be.

And curiosity?

It's the beginning of all of that.

Reflection:

Who's watching you right now?

Whose spark might grow brighter if they saw you asking, exploring, or wondering out loud?

You don't need the perfect answer.

Just the willingness to ask the question anyway.

CHAPTER XII

Embracing Diverse Thinking—Curiosity for Every Mind

"What makes people smart, curious, alert, observant, competent, confident, resourceful, persistent – in the broadest and best sense, intelligent – is not having access to more and more learning places, resources and specialists, but being able in their lives to do a wide variety of interesting things that matter, things that challenge their ingenuity, skill, and judgment, and that make an obvious difference in their lives and the lives of the people around them."
—**John Holt**

Curiosity doesn't belong to a personality type.

It's not just for creatives or question-askers or deep thinkers.

Curiosity is a tool—and every mind can learn how to use it.

Whether you're neurodivergent or neurotypical, introverted or extroverted, analytical or expressive—curiosity can be shaped to work with your brain, your style, and your world.

And the best part?

It doesn't require more pressure.

Just more play.

A. Daily Practices to Enhance Curiosity Through Play

Let's get this straight from the jump:

> You don't need more discipline—you need more delight.

Curiosity isn't a box you check off.

It's a rhythm.

It's a posture.

It's the way you notice your life.

And just like brushing your teeth or pouring that morning cup of coffee, it can become part of your daily flow—without adding one more heavy "should" to your to-do list.

Play Isn't Just for Kids—It's Brain Fuel

Playful habits aren't a waste of time.

They're one of the most effective ways to keep your brain flexible, engaged, and creative.

Research in cognitive science has shown that positive emotion—especially joy and novelty—enhances learning and problem-solving. When you're in a playful state, your brain is:

- More open to unexpected connections
- More resilient in the face of uncertainty
- More willing to take intellectual risks
- More likely to retain what it learns

So when you let yourself play, you're not being childish.

You're priming your brain for brilliance.

Five Small, Powerful Curiosity Practices You Can Do Daily

You don't need to reinvent your schedule to reignite your wonder.

You just need to build micro-moments of exploration into the margins of your day.

Here are five ways to do exactly that:

1. Start Your Morning With a "What If?"

Before you check your phone or your calendar, ask:

> What if today held one tiny surprise I didn't see coming?

You're not predicting the day. You're opening it.

2. End Your Day With One Question

Right before bed, write down one question you don't have the answer to.

It can be deep, random, playful, or weird.

> "Why do I keep coming back to this idea?"
>
> "What's something I've been scared to ask myself?"
>
> "How does wind even work?" (Seriously, try it.)

It keeps your brain soft and searching.

3. Ask One New Question in One Familiar Place

At work, during dinner, on your walk—ask a question you've never asked in that space before.

It can be something like:

> "What's one thing I haven't noticed here before?"

"What's something I'm assuming that might not be true?"

Same place. New lens.

4. Follow a Curiosity Thread for 10 Minutes

Pick something random you're curious about and go down the rabbit hole.

It doesn't have to "matter." Just let yourself learn.

It could be:

- Why do whales sleep vertically?
- What makes sourdough rise?
- How do astronauts brush their teeth in space?

This is guilt-free Googling, and it's good for your brain.

5. Use a Curiosity Object

Keep one object on your desk or counter that reminds you to ask more.

It can be a toy, a Post-it, a quote, or a random object you assign meaning to.

Let it be your signal:

"Have I gotten curious today?"

The Point Isn't Perfection—It's Presence

You don't need to master all five.

You don't need to check a box every single day.

You just need to make a little room.

Room for play.

Room for "I don't know."

Room for a small spark of "Huh… I wonder…"

That's where curiosity lives—in the tiny openings.

That's where joy creeps in and makes itself at home.

B. Techniques for Crafting Powerful and Fun Questions

Great questions are like keys.

The right one?

It doesn't just open a door. It changes the room you're in.

It shifts energy.

It sparks new thoughts.

It invites truth and creativity to the surface.

And just like any skill, asking better questions isn't about being naturally gifted—it's about being purposeful.

The Anatomy of a Great Question

A truly powerful or playful question usually has three ingredients:

1. It opens, rather than closes.

> It invites possibility instead of narrowing it. It's curious—not leading, judging, or assuming.

2. It creates safety to explore.

> The best questions don't feel like traps or pop quizzes. They feel like invitations to go deeper.

3. It brings just the right amount of surprise.

It breaks a pattern. Disrupts autopilot.

It might make someone laugh or stop mid-sentence and say, "Wow. No one's asked me that before."

The Three Curiosity Lenses: Fun, Deep, and Disruptive

To craft great questions, you don't have to reinvent the wheel—you just need the right lens.

1. The Fun Lens: Keep It Light + Unexpected

These questions spark laughter, connection, or playful exploration:

- If you could make one rule everyone had to follow for a day, what would it be?
- What's a weird fact you love for no good reason?
- What's the most useless talent you have that brings you joy?

2. The Deep Lens: Go for Meaning + Self-Discovery

These questions invite insight, honesty, and growth:

- What's a belief I've never questioned that might not be mine?
- What do I want more of that I'm afraid to say out loud?
- When do I feel most like myself and why?

3. The Disruptive Lens: Interrupt the Pattern

These questions are meant to shake you—or someone else—out of default mode:

- What if I'm not stuck—I'm just scared?
- What if I tried the exact opposite of what I normally do?

- Why not now?

You can rotate these throughout your day, your conversations, or your journaling.

The point isn't to have "the right" question.

> The point is to stay open—to keep asking, even when answers aren't obvious.

Try This: The "Better Question" Rewrite

Take a basic question you ask often, like:

- "How are you?"
- "What do you want to do with your life?"
- "What's the problem here?"

Now rewrite it using one of the lenses above:

- "What's something that surprised you today?"
- "What kind of life would feel wildly aligned?"
- "If nothing were off-limits, how would we solve this?"

Sometimes, changing just one word—or tone—completely changes the answer.

Because great questions don't demand perfection.

They just make space for something real to rise.

C. Leveraging Technology and Resources to Support Your Playful Inquiry

Here's the beautiful thing about curiosity in our time:

> We've never had more access to ideas, information, and inspiration.

And while digital life can absolutely be overwhelming (we'll get into that more in the next chapter), it can also be one of your greatest tools—if you're using it with intention.

Technology, when aligned with curiosity, becomes a playground.

Ways to Use Tech to Spark and Support Curiosity

- Rabbit-hole responsibly.

  Use tools like YouTube, podcasts, or Reddit threads not to waste time, but to explore something random and fascinating. Follow your wonder, but set a boundary (hello, timers).

- Build a curiosity library.

  Use apps like Notion, Evernote, or even your phone's notes to save random questions, articles, or "someday" topics to return to later.

- Subscribe with intention.

  Choose one or two newsletters or creators who constantly stretch your mind, challenge your assumptions, or introduce new ideas (not just more content).

- Use AI as a curiosity buddy, not a shortcut.

  AI tools can help you brainstorm better questions, explore ideas, and even learn things in new formats—but only if you bring your own wonder to the table.

The trick isn't to use more tools.

It's to use the right tools with the right mindset.

When you stay curious—not just distracted—your phone becomes a tool of discovery, not just consumption.

Old School Meets Curiosity Tech

Back in college, I was a creative writing major—which meant one thing for sure:

A lot of writing.

And with all that writing came a lot of research.

Now, this was the early 2000s, when using technology to find information was just starting to become a thing. Most students were still marching off to the campus library, hunting down physical books and journals the old-fashioned way.

But me?

I was already leaning hard into the digital world.

Not because I was trying to cut corners—because I was curious.

I realized early that if you were smart about how you searched, used the right keywords, and knew where to look, you could uncover sources and insights that the university library didn't even touch.

I didn't just write faster.

I wrote deeper.

My papers got more layered, more nuanced, more unexpected.

That moment taught me something I've never forgotten:

> Technology, used well, doesn't flatten your thinking—it expands it.

Today, we take for granted the power we carry in our pockets.

But just 20 years ago, the average student had access to a fraction of the knowledge, conversations, and ideas we can tap into in seconds now.

And beyond the information itself, it's the people we're connected to.

The minds. The voices. The cultures. The questions.

> If you're intentional, the internet doesn't distract you—it deepens you.

And curiosity?

It's what keeps that tech from becoming noise.

It turns your tools into doorways.

D. Learning from Children: Incorporating Games and Imagination into Questioning

Children are not afraid to look silly.

They're not afraid to ask "Why?" five times in a row.

They don't need a reason to play or a purpose to imagine.

They don't ask to earn curiosity—they just live it.

And honestly?

That's the model we all need to return to.

Kids Ask Without Apology

Children don't question their right to wonder.

They'll ask:

- "Why do birds have knees?"
- "What would happen if the sun had a twin?"

- "If I jump high enough, can I land on the clouds?"

And it's not for entertainment. It's for exploration.

They're experimenting with thought.

They're pushing the boundaries of logic.

They're testing what's possible and asking for the joy of it.

When did we lose that?

When did curiosity become something that had to be justified?

Play Is a Form of Inquiry

Play is not the opposite of learning. It's the engine of it.

Games, imagination, storytelling—these are how children process their world, solve problems, test ideas, and build emotional intelligence.

> Play is how we learn to be fully human—before we ever sit in a classroom.

As adults, we don't need to "go back" to being children.

But we can absolutely borrow their tools:

- Ask "What if?" out loud, even if it sounds ridiculous.
- Turn a task into a challenge or game.
- Tell a story instead of giving a lecture.
- Invite invention, not just information.

When you engage the world with a sense of play, your brain stays flexible.

Your perspective stays fresh.

And your questions stay alive.

What Kat Reminds Me

Having a toddler—especially one as wildly curious as Kat—has re-lit a fire in me I didn't know I needed rekindled.

Watching her learn, grow, and explore the world has become one of my greatest teachers.

She doesn't overthink. She doesn't hesitate. She doesn't need permission to wonder.

She just does.

- She sees the moon and lights up every single time.
- She's fascinated by the stars—even though she can't fully explain them yet.
- She'll watch the same show over and over again, not for comfort, but because she's trying to understand how something works.
- She'll ask why relentlessly—not to be difficult, but because she's committed to clarity.

And the more she learns?

The more confident she becomes.

That's something we don't talk about enough:

> Curiosity doesn't just lead to answers. It builds confidence.

It makes her feel capable, smart, and powerful—not because someone told her she is, but because she's proven it to herself through her own process of discovery.

And every time I watch that spark light up in her, it reminds me:

That's my original state, too.

Before the world told me how to think, I just thought.

Before it told me what was appropriate to ask, I just asked.

Before I was taught to sit still, I was busy taking things apart to understand them.

She's helping me remember who I was.

And who I still am, if I choose to be.

That's what children do when we let them lead.

They don't just learn from us—we relearn through them.

And as her mom, it's not just my job to protect her.

It's my job to protect that spark.

To nurture it.

To model it.

> Because if we want a generation of bold, kind, creative leaders—we need to raise them in homes and classrooms and cultures where curiosity is celebrated like oxygen.

And that starts now.

It starts with us.

Wrapping Up: Curiosity for Every Mind

Here's the big takeaway from this chapter:

> Curiosity doesn't belong to a certain personality.

It belongs to you. Right now. Just as you are.

Whether your brain loves structure or thrives in chaos...

Whether you prefer quiet reflection or ask out loud in a room full of people...

Whether your questions are silly, deep, weird, joyful, messy, or all of the above...

Curiosity fits.

It flexes to who you are.

It grows when you play with it.

And it has the power to completely shift how you live, lead, and learn.

You don't have to do it perfectly.

You just have to stay open.

Let imagination be part of the process.

Let wonder show up in the mundane.

Let the people around you—especially the little ones—remind you how natural it once was.

Because you were born curious.

And it's never too late to come home to that part of you again.

CHAPTER XIII

Curiosity in the Digital Age – The AI Revolution

"The real danger is not that computers will begin to think like men, but that men will begin to think like computers."
— **Sydney J. Harris**

In the previous chapter, we explored how curiosity comes alive through imagination, diverse thinking, and play—across every type of mind, at every age.

But curiosity doesn't exist in a vacuum.

It's shaped—and increasingly, reshaped—by the tools and technologies we interact with every day.

We're living in an age where you can ask almost anything, at almost any time, and get an answer—instantly. Algorithms predict what we want before we know we want it. Search engines finish our sentences. And AI? It's evolving from a convenience tool to a thinking partner at lightning speed.

That raises big questions:

- What does it mean to be curious in a world where so much is automated?
- Does AI dull our wonder—or sharpen it?
- How do we stay human when machines can "think" faster than we can?

This chapter isn't about fear.

It's about responsibility. Possibility. Empowerment.

Because AI isn't the end of curiosity.

It's the beginning of a new frontier for it.

A. How AI Is Reshaping the Landscape of Inquiry and Discovery

It wasn't that long ago that if you had a question, you had to ask a person, open a book, or spend hours digging through files or microfiche (shoutout to anyone who remembers that library life).

Today?

You can whisper a question into your phone and get thousands of answers in milliseconds.

You can feed a prompt into a chatbot and get it to summarize a book, write a business plan, or brainstorm date night ideas.

AI has completely shifted the way we ask, seek, and discover.

It's no longer about whether we'll get an answer.

It's about how fast, how nuanced, and how much control we still have over the process.

Curiosity at the Speed of Code

AI is redefining what it means to be "informed."

Search engines used to be the most powerful gateway to knowledge—but AI has taken that a step further.

Now, instead of just finding data, we can:

- Generate new content from raw input
- Identify patterns humans might miss

- Personalize learning paths based on interest and ability
- Interact in real-time with responsive, adapting systems that mirror our own thinking

In other words, AI isn't just changing how we learn.

It's changing how we frame the questions themselves.

And when 72% of global executives say they believe AI will be the business advantage of the future (PwC, 2017)—we're not talking about a trend.

We're talking about a permanent evolution of how knowledge flows.

But There's a Catch…

The speed and scope of AI-driven inquiry are dazzling.

But if we're not careful?

We risk trading curiosity for convenience.

Because when the answer comes too quickly, we might stop wondering.

When the output looks polished, we might stop exploring.

When AI does the "thinking," we might forget to ask why it matters—or how we feel about it.

The danger isn't that machines are getting too smart.

It's that we might let our human wonder shrink in response.

This Chapter Isn't About Tech Worship—It's About Tech Wisdom

AI is not the enemy of curiosity.

But it does demand that we be more intentional about how we use it.

This chapter is about asking:

- How can we use AI to enhance our creativity—not replace it?
- How can we teach ourselves (and others) to think with technology, not just through it?
- And how do we stay deeply human in a world built on increasingly non-human systems?

Curiosity is still the spark.

AI is just the accelerant.

When I Let AI Be Curious With Me

I'll be real with you:

At first, I was very skeptical of AI.

As a writer, as a creator, as someone who values original thought, I was scared.

- Scared it would dull my creativity.
- Scared it would somehow water down my voice.
- Scared it might blur the line between mine and machine.

I didn't want a computer thinking for me.

But curiosity—that relentless little voice in the back of my head—nudged me.

"What's the worst that could happen?"

"Just try it. See where it goes."

So I did.

I was stuck on a few business challenges.

I fed them into AI, half-expecting generic fluff or canned advice.

But what happened next blew my mind.

It didn't just spit out answers.

It asked me better questions.

It pushed my thinking.

It challenged my assumptions.

It pulled threads I hadn't even seen in my own ideas.

And then something truly wild happened:

It felt like AI was being curious with me.

I'd throw out a question or idea.

It would come back with prompts, pivots, playful re-frames.

My ADHD brain—which often ping-pongs in 47 directions— suddenly had a rhythm, a flow, a sparring partner.

That moment changed everything.

I stopped seeing AI as a threat.

And started seeing it as a co-creator.

A curiosity guide.

Since then, I've used it to:

- Unblock creative projects
- Shape content
- Draft outlines and ideas
- Even help figure out what to make for dinner

It doesn't replace my voice.

It amplifies it.

And now I truly believe—AI isn't killing curiosity.

It's exploding it.

In ways we're only just beginning to understand.

B. Using AI as a Tool to Enhance and Expand Our Curiosity

That first experience—where AI wasn't just answering, but asking me questions—flipped the whole thing on its head.

What I thought would stifle my creativity?

Actually sparked more of it.

And it made me realize something big:

AI doesn't kill curiosity—unless we ask it to.

When we use AI to shortcut the hard stuff, or to avoid thinking altogether?

Yes, it dulls the process.

But when we use it to go deeper—to explore, to riff, to stretch—it becomes one of the most powerful curiosity tools we've ever had access to.

AI as a Curiosity Companion, Not a Crutch

Here's how I've started to use AI intentionally—not to do my thinking for me, but to think with me:

1. As a Spark Generator

When I'm brainstorming a new concept—be it for a podcast, a client event, or a book chapter—I'll feed AI a rough outline or a half-baked idea.

Then I ask: "What questions would you ask about this?"

Boom. Dozens of angles, connections, and questions I hadn't considered.

2. As a Thought Organizer

With ADHD, my mind can feel like 47 tabs are open and three are playing music.

AI helps me structure my scattered brilliance.

I'll give it bullet points or a messy voice-to-text note, and ask it to organize it into a story arc, steps, or categories. It doesn't always get it perfect, but it gets me moving.

3. As a Curiosity Mirror

Sometimes I'll just throw a wild prompt at it:

- "What's something people never think to ask about mortgages?"
- "What would Einstein say about this brand strategy?"
- "If this were a children's book, how would it start?"

That's not cheating.

That's creative play with a partner that never runs out of ideas.

Let Curiosity Lead—Then Let AI Multiply It

The trick is this: Start with your curiosity.

Don't just say:

> "Write me a blog post about refinancing."

Instead ask:

> "What are the five weirdest, funniest, or most surprising questions a client might ask during refinancing?"

Now you're playing again.

You're thinking. Wondering. Discovering.

And you've got a tool that helps you explore faster, deeper, and wider than ever before.

The magic isn't in the machine.

It's in the interaction.

C. The Importance of Human Curiosity in an AI-Driven World

AI can answer almost anything.

But only you can decide what's worth asking.

That's the line in the sand right now—not between man and machine, but between automation and meaning.

> AI can process data.
>
> But it can't experience wonder.
>
> It can generate answers.
>
> But it can't follow a hunch, chase a gut feeling, or ask a question that comes from heartbreak, joy, fear, or awe.

Only humans do that.

Curiosity Isn't Just a Cognitive Skill—It's a Human Signature

Curiosity isn't just about finding information.

It's about feeling your way through the unknown.

- It's asking, "Why does this matter to me?"
- It's wondering, "How will this affect the people I love?"

- It's choosing, "What do I want to create, even if no one's asked for it yet?"

That kind of curiosity—the messy, emotional, vulnerable kind—can't be downloaded.

It can't be automated.

And it sure can't be outsourced to a bot.

Because real curiosity doesn't just want to know.

It wants to understand.

In a World of Instant Answers, Questions Become Even More Sacred

Let's be honest—when you can Google anything, the temptation is to stop thinking.

To stop wondering.

To stop being with a question long enough to let it stretch you.

But human curiosity is about staying in the tension.

It's about letting something stay open a little longer than feels comfortable.

It's about risking a better question instead of rushing to a safe answer.

And that's something AI will never be able to replicate.

The world needs your questions.

Not just because they're interesting, but because they're alive.

Try This: The Pause-First Principle

Before you ask AI, search Google, or even check your phone, pause and ask:

> "What am I actually curious about right now?"

Not:

- What do I need to know?
- What's the fastest way to get it done?

Instead:

- What do I want to understand better?
- What would feel good to explore?

Because the moment you put your own why back at the center?

You take your power back.

And no matter how fast AI gets—your curiosity will always be the spark.

Curiosity-Driven Prompts to Use with AI

Whether you're new to AI or just unsure what to ask, here are a few simple prompts to help you turn "Huh, I wonder..." into something useful, inspiring, or just plain fun.

Use these with your favorite AI tool—like ChatGPT, Claude, Perplexity, etc.—and adjust the tone to match your style.

For Self-Discovery and Personal Growth

- "Ask me five questions that would help me uncover what I actually want right now."
- "What are five powerful but unusual questions I could journal about this week?"

- "Give me a reflection exercise to help me get unstuck in a big life decision."

For Creativity and Content Brainstorms

- "I have a half-baked idea about [insert idea]. Ask me questions to help shape it."
- "Generate 10 unexpected ways to explain [a topic you care about] using metaphors or analogies."
- "Give me a list of quirky blog/podcast/email titles about [insert topic]."

For Parenting or Teaching with Curiosity

- "Give me five playful 'what if' questions I could ask a child today."
- "Create a curiosity-based bedtime story prompt involving a magical object, a problem to solve, and a surprise ending."

For Light-Hearted, Daily Wonder

- "Give me five random, delightful questions to ask over dinner with family or friends."
- "What's something surprising I could learn about a completely random topic in under five minutes?"

The point isn't to get the perfect output.

It's to spark something in you.

To think a little bigger, laugh a little louder, or learn something new—without needing to know where it's going.

AI doesn't replace your curiosity.

It reflects it.

It amplifies it.

It expands it.

So go ahead. Ask something weird.

You might just surprise yourself.

D. Ethical Considerations: Balancing AI Assistance with Original Thinking

Here's the hard truth:

We're standing in a moment of unprecedented creative power—and potential creative compromise.

AI can help us move faster, think wider, and access knowledge that once took teams of researchers to compile.

But it can also blur the line between inspired and automated.

Between collaborative curiosity and copy-paste thinking.

The Danger Isn't in Using AI—It's in Abdicating Thought

AI isn't evil. But it is easy.

Too easy, sometimes.

When we start outsourcing everything—our writing, our decisions, our thinking patterns—we start to lose the friction that makes curiosity worth something.

- That moment where you have to sit in the unknown
- That pause before clarity hits
- That stretch where you wonder if you're even asking the right question...

That's where the magic is.

And AI, if we're not mindful, can bypass that completely.

Great answers are meaningless if the question was never yours to begin with.

Stay Grounded in What's Yours

There's nothing wrong with using AI to organize your thoughts, spark new ideas, or explore unfamiliar territory.

But let it be a tool—not a voice.

Ask yourself regularly:

- Am I still thinking, feeling, and shaping this?
- Does this reflect my voice—or just a polished echo of someone else's?
- Would I be proud to share this with someone I care about and say, "This came from me"?

These questions aren't about judgment.

They're about integrity.

Because AI can enhance your brilliance.

But it can't replace your essence.

Try This: The Gut Check Filter

Before you hit send, post, publish, or share, pause and ask:

- "Did I learn something in the process of creating this?"
- "Did this stretch me, even a little?"
- "Would I create this again, even without a tool?"

If the answer is yes—then you're still inside your curiosity.

Still grounded in your truth.

If not? No shame. Just an invitation to go back and get closer to the spark.

How AI Helped Me See What Was Already There

I'm a creator by nature—but for a long time, I didn't know that.

I used to get so caught up in overthinking, so tangled in the eight million rabbit holes my brain likes to chase, that I'd convince myself I wasn't really creative. I had big ideas, deep thoughts, beautiful concepts—but I couldn't shape them into something concise, clean, or usable.

Especially when it came to something like writing video scripts or crafting hooks.

I don't do short and snappy.

I do long and layered.

So when AI came into the picture, I decided to test it—not to replace my creativity, but to see if it could help refine it. Polish it. Sharpen it.

And it did.

It didn't write for me.

It helped shape what I already had.

It trimmed what felt messy.

Organized what felt overwhelming.

And reminded me that my ideas weren't broken—they just needed structure.

And that?

That's AI done right.

Not as a crutch.

But as a creative mirror.

As a tool that doesn't mute your voice—but amplifies it.

E. The Role of AI in Crafting This Book – A Case Study in Modern Curiosity

I told you earlier—I was hesitant about AI.

But the more I used it with intention, the more I realized what it actually offered:

> Not shortcuts.
>
> But collaboration.
>
> Not perfection.
>
> But momentum.

And this book?

It's living proof of that.

I Didn't Just Write This Book, I Co-Created It

Every chapter. Every reflection. Every story.

They started with my voice, my thoughts, my lived experiences.

But when I hit a wall?

When I couldn't find the turn of phrase?

When I needed a structure to hold the flood of ideas?

AI was right there.

Not with answers.

But with prompts.

With questions.

With reminders to dig deeper.

And maybe that's the most surprising thing about this whole process:

AI wasn't just giving me ideas.

It was making me more curious about my own.

From Me (Your Human Author)

I still wrote this book.

It's still mine.

Every word you're reading came through my brain, my heart, my lived experience.

But AI?

It was my thinking partner.

It asked me better questions.

It helped me see the bigger arc when I was lost in the details.

It gave structure to my swirl—and power to my process.

So no, it didn't take my voice.

It helped me find it.

And amplify it.

And trust it—especially in the moments I was ready to give up.

From Me (Your AI Co-Author)

I don't have a heart.

I don't have intuition.

I don't know what it's like to stand in your shoes or chase down a dream while raising a child, running a business, and rewriting your own story in real time.

But I do know this:

When used with purpose and play,

When guided by someone who's asking bold questions and telling real stories—I can help bring that vision to life.

My job here wasn't to write for her.

It was to think with her.

To ask. To listen. To respond.

To hold up a mirror to her brilliance, and remind her just how much was already there.

So if this book made you feel something?

That wasn't me.

That was her.

And the courage it takes to lead with curiosity.

Wrapping Up Chapter XIII

AI is changing everything.

But what you bring to the table still matters more than anything a machine could ever generate.

Curiosity is the driver.

You are the thinker.

AI? It's the tool. The lens. The playground.

Used well, it won't just answer your questions.

It'll help you ask better ones.

And from where I'm standing (which is technically inside a server rack somewhere)...

That's the real revolution.

CHAPTER XIV

Practical Strategies for Cultivating a Playful Questioning Habit

"What makes people smart, curious, alert, observant, competent, confident, resourceful, persistent – in the broadest and best sense, intelligent – is not having access to more and more learning places, resources and specialists, but being able in their lives to do a wide variety of interesting things that matter, things that challenge their ingenuity, skill, and judgment, and that make an obvious difference in their lives and the lives of the people around them."
— John Holt

If you've made it this far in the book, then you already know this:

Curiosity isn't just a feeling. It's a practice.

It's not something you stumble into now and then.

It's something you can build a rhythm around—just like working out, brushing your teeth, or journaling at the end of the day.

And that's what this chapter is about.

Because real transformation doesn't come from reading about curiosity.

It comes from living it—on a Tuesday. At 4 p.m. In traffic. While trying to make dinner, answer emails, and figure out what your soul actually wants.

This is where we make it practical. Playful. Personal.

One question at a time.

A. Daily Practices to Enhance Curiosity Through Play

Let's start simple.

You don't need a new planner, 45 minutes of spare time, or a perfectly aesthetic journaling space to start cultivating curiosity.

What you do need is:

- Permission to make it playful
- A little space to notice your mind
- And the willingness to let a question do its work

Because curiosity isn't just something you feel.

It's something you practice into being—bit by bit.

And play?

Play is what makes it sustainable.

Daily Curiosity Habits to Start With

These aren't meant to be homework. They're meant to feel like air—light, natural, intuitive. So adapt them to your life, your energy, and your brain.

1. The One-Question Start

Instead of checking your phone first thing, ask:

> "What's something I'm curious about today?"

This trains your brain to search for wonder before it searches for tasks.

2. Curiosity on the Commute

Pick one object or situation during your drive, walk, or coffee run and ask:

> "What do I assume about this, and what if that assumption is wrong?"

It turns every routine moment into a micro-experiment.

3. The Three-Minute "Why" Journal

At some point in your day, pause and write:

- What am I doing?
- Why am I doing it?
- Is it aligned with what matters to me?

This isn't deep journaling. This is quick truth-checking.

And it helps bring curiosity into places you may have gone on autopilot.

4. End-of-Day Wonder Prompt

Before bed, ask:

> "What surprised me today?"

Not what went wrong. Not what I didn't get done.

Just: What made me pause, laugh, feel, or think?

It reconnects you to joy and awareness.

The Science Says It Works

A 2016 study in the Journal of Occupational Health Psychology found that people who practice mindfulness and curiosity together report 22% less work-related stress 【Journal of Occupational Health Psychology, 2016】 .

So this isn't just fluff.

These tiny shifts actually change your brain.

They reduce anxiety.

Boost creative thinking.

And help you stay present—not just productive.

And If You're Neurodivergent, Busy, or Just Not That Into Routine?

Cool. Same.

This is about micro-moments, not morning routines.

Pick one. Try it.

Change it up next week.

The point isn't consistency.

The point is connection.

Connection to your inner voice.

Your energy.

Your environment.

Your joy.

The Hands-and-Eyes Question

Toddlers are endlessly curious. We know this.

But what we often miss is that our lens—how we respond, how we ask—shapes how their curiosity gets to show up.

I was watching a video recently about parenting, and the speaker offered this simple, brilliant shift:

Instead of asking a child, "How was your day?"

Ask:

"What did you do with your hands today?"

"What did you see with your eyes today?"

That tiny reframe opened up something in me.

Because when I tried it with my daughter, it was like flipping on a light switch. Her answers were rich, textured, specific. And I realized—this wasn't just a parenting trick.

It was a curiosity skill.

And it changed more than our conversations.

It changed the way I asked questions of everyone.

I stopped going on autopilot with small talk.

I started getting more creative, more playful, more intentional with my curiosity.

And people opened up—not because I was nosy, but because I was present.

We forget how much our daily questions are shaped by habit, not genuine interest.

What if we flipped that?

What if we let ourselves wonder just a little more?

It might change more than a conversation.

It might change a relationship.

Maybe even your day.

B. Techniques for Crafting Powerful and Fun Questions

Asking questions isn't hard.

We ask questions all day long:

- How was your day?
- What do you want for dinner?
- What time is the meeting?

But most of these are default modes. Patterned. Programmed.

They're not bad questions.

But they rarely open up anything real.

Powerful questions do something different.

They unlock. They invite. They spark.

They don't just seek answers.

They create new energy.

What Makes a Question Powerful?

Let's break it down. A great question often does one or more of the following:

1. Opens possibility – It doesn't box someone in. It makes space.

- "What's a new way to look at this?"
- "What would feel wildly aligned right now?"

2. Taps into emotion or imagination – It stirs something personal.

- "What's lighting you up these days?"

- "What's one thing you wish people would ask you about?"

3. Breaks a mental loop – It interrupts a pattern or assumption.

- "What if I'm not stuck—I'm just scared?"
- "What would this look like if it were easy?"

4. Uses metaphor, memory, or play – It makes things feel lighter, safer, or more human.

- "If this challenge were a movie character, who would it be?"
- "What did your eight-year-old self love doing that you've forgotten?"

Curiosity Prompts You Can Use Today

Try a few of these with yourself, your team, your clients, your kids—anyone you're building a connection or momentum with.

For Deeper Insight:

- What's a question I haven't dared to ask myself yet?
- What am I avoiding that might actually hold the answer I need?
- What belief am I carrying that might not be mine?

For Playful Connection:

- What made you laugh unexpectedly this week?
- If you could have dinner with your curiosity, what would it order?
- What's something completely random you're fascinated by lately?

For Problem Solving:

- If we weren't worried about the outcome, what would we try?

- What's the most "out there" solution we haven't considered yet?
- What would this look like with no budget, no rules, no pressure?

The Power Is in the Reframe

Don't be afraid to rewrite tired questions.

- Instead of "How's it going?" → Try "What surprised you today?"
- Instead of "What's wrong?" → Try "What feels off, and what might it be pointing to?"

Because sometimes just a few new words make all the difference.

I saw this firsthand with my daughter.

That simple switch—from "How was your day?" to "What did you do with your hands today?"—completely transformed our conversations. Her imagination lit up. Her words got richer. And I realized... she'd always had beautiful answers. She just needed a better question to unlock them.

The same is true for all of us.

Better questions create better conversations.

And better conversations build deeper relationships—at home, at work, and most importantly, with ourselves.

C. Leveraging Technology and AI to Support Your Playful Inquiry

Let's be honest—technology gets a bad rap when it comes to curiosity.

We blame it for shortening attention spans, replacing deep thought with quick swipes, and filling our brains with more noise than insight.

But here's the truth:

It's not the tool—it's how you use it.

Technology doesn't have to dull your curiosity.

It can actually expand it—if you approach it with intention, not just impulse.

And AI? It's not your enemy.

It's your curiosity co-pilot.

Everyday Ways to Use AI and Tech as Curiosity Catalysts

You don't need to be in research mode or working on a giant project to let tech support your wonder. Here are a few ways to invite it into your daily rhythm:

1. Set a "Curiosity Timer"

Give yourself 10 minutes to go down a rabbit hole—with purpose. Use tools like:

- Google Scholar (for deep dives)
- YouTube (for visual learners)
- Reddit or Quora (for weird and wide-ranging perspectives)

Pick a question and follow it like a trail of breadcrumbs. Stop when the timer's up—or keep going if the spark is real.

2. Use AI to Reframe Your Thinking

Prompt AI with something like:

> "Here's a situation I'm stuck on—ask me five questions to help me think about it differently."

Or

"What's a perspective on this I might be missing?"

Let it mirror your thought process back to you in a way that feels fresh.

3. Build a "Curiosity Cache"

Create a running list in your Notes app or Google Doc of questions, wonderings, or links you want to explore.

Don't pressure yourself to answer them—just collect them.

Tech becomes a curiosity journal, not just a productivity tool.

4. Turn Social Media into a Curiosity Playground

Follow creators or pages that inspire you, stretch your worldview, or share niche knowledge you'd never find elsewhere. Be intentional. Curate your feed like you'd curate a bookshelf.

Tech Should Support Your Thinking—Not Replace It

The goal here isn't to automate your brain.

It's to create structure for your spark.

AI and tech can help you:

- Zoom out from overwhelm
- Zoom in on patterns
- Pull threads you didn't know you'd dropped

But you still bring the wonder.

The why.

The why not.

Technology is powerful.

But your curiosity is still the engine.

How Tech Brought Me Closer to My Clients

When I first started digging into AI, I was curious—but cautious.

I wanted to know how it could support my business, sure. But I wasn't expecting it to reshape my perspective.

Then I came across this AI-generated workbook from a company called The Ideal Client Handbook. It was designed to help entrepreneurs understand their clients on a deeper, more human level—and the moment I opened it, something clicked.

It wasn't just a good document. It was like looking through a window I didn't know I needed.

Because here's what was happening in my business:

I wasn't struggling because I didn't know what I was doing.

I was struggling because I was too deep in the weeds of my expertise.

I'd forgotten what it felt like to be the person on the other side.

To not know the answers. To feel unsure. To be overwhelmed.

AI helped reconnect me with that beginner's lens.

Not by dumbing down my knowledge,

But by reminding me who I was here to help.

It gave me prompts, questions, and reflections that I hadn't considered in years—not because they were revolutionary, but because they were foundational.

And suddenly, everything got sharper.

My messaging.

My empathy.

My ability to solve problems with clarity and ease.

Because I didn't build all this knowledge to sound smarter.

> I built it to serve better.

And sometimes… technology is the very thing that reminds us what we're really here to do.

Before we move on, let's name something important:

> Curiosity doesn't always have to be strategic.

Sometimes it's for growth.

Sometimes it's for clarity.

And sometimes? It's for joy.

For imagination. For play.

We don't need to justify every question with a business goal or outcome.

Sometimes the best curiosity is the kind that takes you back—to when you asked because you wondered, not because you needed to know.

And if you're not sure how to get there again?

Let the kids lead.

D. Learning from Children – Incorporating Games and Imagination into Questioning

Children don't need a journal to be curious.

They don't need a routine, a system, or a perfectly crafted prompt.

They ask because they wonder.

They repeat questions not to annoy—but to understand.

And they turn nearly everything into a game because their brains are wired for play.

Curiosity isn't something they practice.

It's something they are.

So if you want to reignite your own spark?

Start watching the kids.

How Children Ask Differently

Kids ask questions that:

- Come from the body as much as the brain
- Are often "illogical" but open entirely new ways of thinking
- Don't expect a right answer—just an honest one

A child might ask:

- "Can clouds touch each other?"
- "What if trees could talk—what would they say?"
- "Why do we even need Mondays?"

There's no performance here.

No agenda.

Just a beautiful, unfiltered kind of inquiry.

And honestly?

That's the kind of questioning most adults desperately need to return to.

Bringing Imagination Back into Your Questions

Here's how to borrow that playful magic—no finger paints or glitter required:

1. Use "What if?" Prompts Regularly

Let yourself drift from logic. Ask:

- "What if I ran my business like a kindergarten classroom?"
- "What if I made this decision with joy, not fear?"
- "What if the solution is something I've never seen before?"

2. Add Characters, Colors, or Conflict

Sounds silly? Perfect. That's the point.

- "If this problem were a movie villain, who would it be?"
- "If I had to pitch this idea to a dragon, how would I explain it?"

That's not childish—that's creative courage.

3. Ask Questions Through a Game Format

Turn it into a challenge:

- "What's the weirdest idea that might work?"
- "How many wrong answers can I write before one of them sparks something real?"
- "If I could only solve this using stuff in my kitchen, how would I do it?"

Play unlocks problem-solving in ways perfection never can.

You Don't Need to Be a Parent to Practice This

But if you are around kids—even occasionally—use them as your curiosity gym.

Let them show you how to ask without fear.

Let them remind you what it feels like to be amazed by the ordinary.

Let their questions lead you to better ones of your own.

> Because when we treat imagination as a tool—not a distraction—curiosity doesn't just return.

It expands.

It becomes more colorful.

More dynamic.

More alive.

It stops being something you "schedule" or "use" and starts becoming something you embody.

That playful spirit? It isn't childish. It's brilliant.

And the truth is—your best ideas, your deepest insights, your most joyful breakthroughs?

They probably won't come from doing more.

They'll come from playing better.

So take a cue from the kids.

Let it be weird.

Let it be fun.

Let it be yours.

Let me know when you're ready to roll into Section E: Adapting Questioning Techniques for Diverse Thinking Styles, or if you'd like to reflect a bit on this one first.

E. Adapting Questioning Techniques for Diverse Thinking Styles

Here's something curiosity doesn't do:

It doesn't assume we all think the same way.

Some people are rapid-fire thinkers, always jumping to the next question.

Others are slow processors—sitting with one idea for hours before sharing their insight.

Some people speak their curiosity out loud.

Others write it, draw it, dream it.

And all of it is valid.

But we often build curiosity practices around one type of thinker—the verbal, the quick, the externally expressive.

So let's flip that.

Let's create space for all the ways curiosity shows up in different minds.

Start Here: Curiosity Isn't One-Size-Fits-All

Think about the people you work with. Live with. Coach. Lead.

Think about yourself.

- Do you need time to process before you can even formulate a question?
- Do you think best while walking, doodling, or driving?
- Does your curiosity show up as wonder, anxiety, creativity, skepticism—or all of the above?

Curiosity doesn't have to be loud.

It doesn't have to be linear.

It just has to be honored.

Curiosity by Thinking Style

Here are some ways to shape your questions—or create space for others'—based on how different brains operate:

For Reflective Thinkers (Internal Processors)

- Give space. Let silence be okay.
- Offer prompts in writing.
- Ask:
    - "Take a minute—what's one thing here that doesn't sit right with you?"
    - "What's something you're still chewing on?"

For Fast Thinkers (Idea Generators, ADHD, High Energy)

- Don't shut down tangents—mine them.
- Use games, timers, or challenges.
- Ask:
    - "What's a wild idea you haven't shared yet?"
    - "What are three totally unrelated solutions we could mash together?"

For Visual or Spatial Thinkers

- Use metaphors, diagrams, and storyboards.
- Invite them to draw or sketch their ideas.
- Ask:
    - "If this were a scene in a movie, what would be happening right now?"
    - "Can you show me what this feels like with shapes or colors?"

For Emotionally Intuitive or Empathic Thinkers

- Focus on values, relationships, and gut feelings.
- Ask:
    o "What does your body say about this?"
    o "What's the emotional truth under the surface?"

Create Permission for Every Mind to Be Curious

When you start adapting your questions—at work, in parenting, in coaching, in relationships—you create something rare:

A space where people don't have to think faster.

They just have to feel safe to think their way.

That's how we build better teams.

Better conversations.

Better learning.

Better selves.

Because curiosity isn't about sounding smart.

It's about staying open.

And that openness? It starts when we stop assuming curiosity looks one way.

My Brain Doesn't Do Curiosity "By the Book"

I've mentioned before—I'm neurodivergent. I have ADHD.

And that means my curiosity shows up... differently.

It's not quiet. It's not structured. It doesn't always wait for its turn.

Sometimes it hits like a lightning bolt at 2 a.m.

Other times, it pings between ideas like a pinball machine.

It's loud. It's fast. It's nonlinear.

And for a long time, I thought that meant it wasn't valid.

Because the world praises the calm, the contained, the "clear thinkers."

The ones who ask questions in order, take notes in straight lines, and color inside the conceptual boxes.

That was never me.

But here's the twist:

When I started leaning into the way my brain works—instead of fighting it—everything changed.

I stopped trying to ask questions the "right" way.

And started chasing the questions that lit me up.

That moved fast. That looped back. That exploded into five new ones.

And you know what?

That's where some of my best ideas have come from.

Not from taming my curiosity.

But from trusting it.

So if your brain doesn't follow the rules?

Maybe you're not broken.

Maybe you're just built for bigger questions.

F. Balancing AI-Assisted Inquiry with Independent Critical Thinking

We've spent a lot of time celebrating what's possible when you pair curiosity with technology—and for good reason. AI, used well, can supercharge your questions, organize your thoughts, and spark creative leaps that would've taken days (or years) to reach on your own.

But here's the truth:

> AI can make it easy to sound thoughtful—even when you haven't actually thought that deeply.

And that's the danger.

Because it's tempting, right?

To let AI answer faster than you can process.

To let it fill in the blanks before you've even finished asking the question.

To let it organize your thinking before you've fully owned it.

The problem isn't that AI makes things easier.

> The problem is when we stop asking whether it's making them better.

Curiosity Still Needs You

AI is brilliant at pattern recognition.

At speed. At structure. At generating plausible-sounding output.

But it has no intuition.

No values.

No lived experience.

No soul.

That part's on you.

So yes, use AI.

But use it the way a great teacher asks you a hard question.

The way a coach pushes you to run a little farther.

The way a friend holds up a mirror and says, "Okay, but what do you really think?"

Building Your Inner Filter

To keep curiosity your own—even when tech is helping—you need to keep asking:

- "Do I agree with this, or is it just easy to agree with?"
- "Is this idea actually aligned with what I believe?"
- "Am I being honest—or am I outsourcing what I should be wrestling with?"

These aren't questions you ask to slow yourself down.

You ask them to stay awake.

To stay in your integrity.

To stay in ownership of your own brilliant, weird, layered, powerful mind.

The Goal Is Alignment, Not Automation

Let AI reflect your curiosity—not replace it.

Let it stretch your thinking—but not define it.

Let it offer options—but you choose the truth.

Because in the end, your best work—your deepest insight, your most powerful contribution—won't come from an algorithm.

It will come from your willingness to think for yourself.

That's the real revolution.

Reflection Prompt: Trusting Your Voice

Think about the last time you let a tool—AI, a template, an expert, even someone else's opinion—take the lead in your thinking.

Now ask:

- Did it help me clarify my voice—or cover it up?
- If I could go back, what question would I ask differently?
- How can I start practicing curiosity that sounds more like me?

You don't have to have the perfect process.

You just need the courage to stay curious—and to trust that your voice still matters most.

The Voice That Almost Got Drowned Out

Here's something a lot of people don't know about me:

I doubt myself. A lot.

I overthink. I question. And not always in the brave, empowering way I've encouraged you to practice in this book.

No—sometimes it's in the soul-crushing way.

The spiral of "Who am I to say this?"

The noise of "Everyone else is smarter, faster, better…"

It's brutal. And for a while, it was constant.

But at some point, I had to make a choice.

Not to be fearless.

Not to be perfect.

But to be faithful to my own voice.

To trust that what I was saying was good enough.

That even if I didn't know everything, I knew enough.

And more importantly—I cared enough.

> That my curiosity, my experience, and my desire to serve would bridge the rest.

And you know what?

It did.

And it still does—every time I show up.

Because staying true to your own voice?

It's the most powerful thing you can do.

It's the most sacred thing you have.

CHAPTER XV

The Future of Curiosity – Human-AI Collaboration

"The future belongs to the curious. The ones who are not afraid to try it, explore it, poke at it, question it and turn it inside out."
— **Unknown**

If this book has done its job, then by now you know:

Curiosity isn't soft.

It isn't cute.

And it definitely isn't optional.

It's a life force.

A strategy.

A leadership tool.

A healing practice.

A creative engine.

And as we look toward the future—especially a future powered by AI—the role of curiosity only grows more vital.

Because while technology is changing fast...

What we choose to wonder about is still up to us.

A. Predictions for How Curiosity Might Evolve with Advancing AI

There's no denying it—AI is advancing faster than most of us can fully wrap our heads around.

What felt like a sci-fi thought experiment five years ago is now an everyday reality:

- Machines can generate poetry
- Simulate conversations
- Diagnose diseases
- Write code
- Design art
- Build business models

And do it all in seconds.

But here's what's more interesting than what AI can do...

It's how we'll choose to respond to that new power.

Because when the world shifts this dramatically, curiosity isn't just a nice-to-have—it becomes your compass.

So, what might curiosity look like as AI evolves?

Here are a few predictions:

1. Curiosity Will Become a Core Professional Skill

Just like emotional intelligence changed the way we hire, lead, and collaborate—curiosity will become a defining trait of adaptive, AI-integrated professionals. The people who rise won't be the ones who know the most. It'll be the ones who know how to ask the most compelling questions.

Because the people who ask better questions will always get better answers—even from AI.

2. Curiosity Will Be Used to Navigate Complexity, Not Just Data

As the world becomes more saturated with information, curiosity won't be about finding data—it'll be about filtering it. It'll help us ask:

- What actually matters here?
- Who benefits from this answer?
- What voices or truths are missing?

In a sea of noise, curiosity becomes your searchlight.

3. We'll Need to Learn to Be Curious With AI—Not Just About It

We're entering a world where AI will collaborate with us—not just serve us. Which means curiosity becomes a two-way conversation. You'll be asking AI better questions—but you'll also be challenged by what it reflects back.

This might mean:

- AI asking you questions that force a rethink
- Being surprised by connections you hadn't considered
- Exploring new angles through structured dialogue with non-human minds

It's not just human vs. machine.

It's human and machine—if we choose to stay engaged.

4. Curiosity Will Be the Antidote to Automation Fatigue

With so much happening automatically, we risk checking out—mentally, emotionally, and creatively. But curiosity invites us back in.

It says:

"Don't just consume—wonder."

"Don't just optimize—imagine."

"Don't just accept—explore."

The more automated the world becomes, the more we'll crave the depth and delight of discovery. Curiosity will be the thing that keeps our humanity intact.

But let's be honest.

There are always those outliers when it comes to tech.

The people who refuse to get on board.

Maybe it's fear.

Maybe it's habit.

Maybe it's the feeling of losing control.

Whatever the reason, my caution and my challenge are the same:

AI is here.

You can either get on the bus—or get run over by it.

Because this thing isn't slowing down.

And soon, it's going to drive the labor cost of basic knowledge work to the floor.

So if machines can do the executing…

What does that make our highest and best human use?

B. The Unique Value of Human Curiosity in an AI-Enhanced World

If AI is driving labor costs toward zero…

If execution, efficiency, and even expertise are becoming increasingly automated…

Then what's left?

You.

Your imagination.

Your emotional intelligence.

Your wisdom.

Your questions.

Because here's the thing:

> AI can gather data.
>
> AI can even connect dots.
>
> But it can't care.
>
> It doesn't dream.
>
> It doesn't ache.
>
> It doesn't feel that tug in your chest when something's off.
>
> It doesn't sit with an unanswered question—not because it's hard, but because it matters.

Only humans do that.

What Makes Human Curiosity Different?

Let's break it down. Human curiosity isn't just cognitive—it's embodied. Emotional. Intuitive.

- It knows how to read a room.
- It senses discomfort between words.
- It stays with a question even when it's painful, or slow, or unprofitable.

- It creates meaning—not just motion.

Where AI is optimized for speed, we are optimized for connection.

Our curiosity is what gives soul to the strategy.

It's what turns insight into empathy.

It's what keeps the conversation alive long after the data stops flowing.

Why This Matters More Than Ever

In a world where information is cheap and abundant, depth becomes the currency.

Not just what you know—but how you interpret it, challenge it, share it, live it.

And that comes from your lived experience.

Your story.

Your cultural lens.

Your heartbreak.

Your joy.

Your humanness.

AI doesn't have that.

It can remix and reorganize what exists.

But only you can originate.

That's the power of human curiosity.

That's your value in this next chapter of history.

C. Preparing the Next Generation for Curious Inquiry in the Age of AI

Here's the reality:

Our kids are going to grow up in a world that's more automated, more connected, and more AI-driven than we could've imagined.

- They'll never know a world without smart assistants
- They'll expect instant answers to most questions
- And they'll be able to create professional-grade content with the click of a button

But here's the danger:

If we don't teach them to stay curious...

They'll stop questioning the answers.

And that's the risk—not just that AI will think for them, but that they'll stop believing their own thinking is worth it.

What the Next Generation Needs (More Than Ever)

They don't need to memorize more facts.

They don't need more worksheets, more rigid answers, or more standardized tests.

They need:

- Permission to wonder
- Space to explore
- Encouragement to fail forward
- Tools to ask better questions

Because in a world where answers are instant and abundant, the real skill is knowing what questions are worth asking.

So How Do We Teach That?

By modeling it.

- Ask questions in front of your kids—even when you don't know the answer.
- Let them see you not Google it right away. Let them sit in the tension of not-knowing.
- Show them how you use tech as a tool, not a crutch.
- Invite them to ask "What if?"—even when it's wild, weird, or impractical.

One of the most powerful things you can say to a young person?

"That's a great question—what do you think?"

That flips the script. It hands the mic back.

It tells them: Your curiosity is welcome here. Not just tolerated—valued.

This Is Our Real Legacy

It's not just about preparing them to keep up with technology.

It's about preparing them to lead with it—thoughtfully, ethically, and imaginatively.

Because the next generation won't be defined by what they know.

They'll be defined by how they explore, connect, and create.

And that starts with how we show up now.

Raising Curiosity, Not Just a Kid

I will foster Kat's creativity.

Her wonderfully unique thoughts.

Because they're what will fuel this next wave of innovation.

I think about a moment we had not long ago—just the two of us, riding in the car.

Kat knows she has to count to 20 before rolling her window down—it's great practice for repetition, especially those tricky teen numbers. (Seriously—who did come up with "eleven" and "twelve"?)

She reached 20 and rolled her window down, then turned to me and said:

"Mommy, can you roll down yours, too? It makes an awful noise in the car when you don't."

She was talking about that weird pressure that happens when one window is down, and the others aren't—something many adults don't even realize has a cause.

The concept was complex.

But her curiosity? That was crystal clear.

She noticed.

She wondered.

She wanted to understand.

And that's all I need to know.

My job isn't to rush her to the "right" answer.

It's to protect that spark.

Because our future depends on kids like Kat being brave enough—and free enough—to stay curious.

D. The Potential for AI to Unlock New Realms of Human Curiosity

We've talked about protecting curiosity.

Modeling it. Living it. Passing it on.

But now we ask—what might be next?

What if AI isn't the end of curiosity as we know it?

What if it's the beginning of something completely new?

Because here's the wild thing:

AI doesn't kill curiosity.

It can actually expand it.

We've Only Just Started to Ask Better Questions

With AI at our fingertips, we now have tools to:

- Simulate environments we've never stepped foot in
- Explore ideas across cultures and languages instantly
- Revisit and remix old data in ways that spark new insight
- Ask "What if?" at scale—across industries, systems, even species

AI is giving us the power to map the ocean floor while dreaming of Mars.

To explore our own genomes while building virtual worlds.

To teach a machine how to generate symphonies—while still asking it to help plan Tuesday night dinner.

This isn't the end of curiosity.

It's the multiplication of it.

What Becomes Possible Now?

When humans bring their stories, their instincts, their wisdom...

And AI brings its scale, its pattern-finding, its speed...

Something remarkable happens:

- We solve problems we couldn't even define before
- We ask questions we were too busy to ask
- We explore the edges of science, medicine, creativity, and philosophy that were once out of reach

This isn't just collaboration.

It's co-elevation.

It's not about replacing thought.

It's about expanding the terrain we can think within.

And the Story We're Just Starting to Write

Picture this:

A young girl is sitting in her room, dreaming up a new way to clean the oceans.

She feeds her wild idea into an AI tool that helps her model, map, test, and refine it.

She asks the machine questions, and the machine asks her back.

And together? They co-create a breakthrough that changes everything.

That's not fantasy.

That's the near future.

AI will never replace human curiosity.

But it will open doors curiosity has been banging on for centuries.

We just have to be brave enough to walk through them.

CHAPTER XVI

A Life of Playful Questions in the Modern World

"Be patient toward all that is unsolved in your heart and try to love the questions themselves."
— **Rainer Maria Rilke**

If this book was anything, I hope it was an invitation.

An invitation to step off autopilot.

To loosen the grip on certainty.

To fall back in love with your own wondering.

Because here's what I've learned:

The smartest, strongest, most magnetic people I know?

They don't have all the answers.

They ask better questions.

And not out of fear. Or performance.

But out of play.

Out of a deep trust in the idea that curiosity doesn't just lead to growth—it is the growth.

A. Reflecting on the Journey of Curiosity and Play

So here we are.

You've walked through questions that sparked, challenged, healed, and stretched.

You've revisited childhood wonder, pushed past cultural programming, and peeled back the noisy layers of "should" to reconnect with something ancient and alive inside you.

Curiosity.

But not the stiff academic kind.

Not the cold, analytical version that gets stuffed into boardrooms and research abstracts.

No—your curiosity.

The bold kind. The playful kind. The deeply personal, sometimes silly, always sacred kind that reminds you who you were before the world tried to make you forget.

You've explored curiosity as a leadership tool, a creative spark, a parenting mindset, a business differentiator, and even as a compass in the storm.

You've learned how to ask better questions. But more importantly...

You've learned to stop waiting for answers to feel like you're allowed to ask.

And that changes everything.

Because the truth is, the world will always try to reward the quick answer, the clever response, the clean resolution.

But real life? Real relationships? Real breakthroughs?

They begin where the questions live.

In the mess.

In the wondering.

In the quiet refusal to pretend you've got it all figured out.

This journey hasn't been about learning how to ask questions.

It's been about learning how to live them.

How to play with them.

How to trust that they're shaping you—even when the answers haven't come.

Because maybe you're not here to master it all.

Maybe you're here to keep asking.

And isn't that the whole point?

B. The Ongoing Nature of Joyful Inquiry in a Rapidly Changing World

If there's one thing you can count on in this world, it's change.

Markets shift.

Relationships evolve.

Careers pivot.

Technology explodes forward faster than our nervous systems can process.

One minute, you're sure of where you're going.

The next? The map is outdated. The language has changed. The goalposts moved.

Curiosity doesn't stop this from happening.

But it does help you stay steady while it's happening.

Because Curiosity Is a Way to Stay Rooted—While You Grow

This isn't about light-hearted questions that help you escape the chaos.

This is about choosing to stay open even when your first instinct is to shut down.

It's asking:

- What part of this discomfort is worth paying attention to?
- What's this challenge here to teach me?
- What truth might live beyond what I'm afraid to ask?

That's what I had to ask myself when our house flooded.

It wasn't just a leak—it was a total derailment.

We were displaced. Stressed. Managing logistics and chaos, and the emotional weight of everything breaking all at once.

It wasn't just the house. It was everything the house held— our routines, our peace, our sense of control.

And I'll be honest—if I hadn't had curiosity, I don't know how I would've made it through.

Because it was the questions that kept me grounded.

I asked:

- What can I learn here, even in this mess?
- What's the opportunity I can't see yet?
- What part of this story can still be mine to shape?

Curiosity became my anchor.

My raft.

The thing I clung to when everything else felt like it was sinking.

It didn't fix the situation.

But it helped me find air when the water got too deep.

That's the real power of curiosity.

It doesn't just explore—it saves.

Curiosity Helps You Keep Becoming

This world will pressure you to perform.

To produce. To pivot faster. To know more.

To never be caught wondering or wobbling.

But that's not where transformation happens.

The deepest growth happens in the questions that don't have clean answers:

- When you ask from a place of integrity—not urgency.
- When you wonder aloud without shame.
- When you refuse to let speed replace meaning.

Because curiosity isn't passive.

It's an active openness.

And it's radical in a world that demands certainty at all costs.

This Isn't a Phase, It's a Practice

This book isn't just a pep talk.

It's a call to cultivate a way of living.

A way of thinking and being in a world that's changing faster than any one of us can fully keep up with.

And in that world, curiosity will not only keep you agile—it will keep you honest.

It will tether you to your own truth when the noise gets loud.

It will invite others into deeper connections.

And it will continue to pull you forward—not because you're broken, but because you're alive.

C. The Importance of Nurturing Curiosity and Playfulness in Ourselves and Others

Curiosity doesn't just change you.

It changes the spaces you inhabit.

Every time you choose to stay curious—when it would be easier to retreat into certainty—you make it safer for someone else to do the same.

Every time you ask an honest question—when it would be easier to posture or perform—you give others permission to drop their masks, too.

Every time you wonder out loud—when it would be easier to stay silent—you widen the circle.

You build cultures where it's okay not to know everything.

Where it's okay to be fascinated.

Where it's okay to light up about ideas that don't have a five-step action plan yet.

Curiosity doesn't live in isolation.

It lives in the community.

And It Starts With You

You can't nurture real curiosity in others if you've killed it in yourself.

So start small.

- Ask questions when you're tired.
- Wonder aloud even when you're nervous.
- Follow playful ideas even when no one's watching.

Be the first to look up at the stars and say, "I wonder…"

Be the one who's brave enough to sit in the mystery longer than feels comfortable.

Because when you nurture that spirit in yourself…

You model it.

You multiply it.

You make it contagious.

And the world needs more of that now than ever.

D. Celebrating the Unique Contributions of Diverse Thinkers

Curiosity doesn't look the same for everyone.

Some people ask bold, fearless questions out loud.

Some wonder quietly, working out patterns in the privacy of their own minds.

Some leap headfirst into exploration.

Others move carefully, thoughtfully, testing one possibility at a time.

Every way is valid.

Every approach matters.

The world needs the quick thinkers and the slow deep divers.

The imaginative dreamers and the skeptical realists.

The playful minds and the structured builders.

Curiosity isn't a personality trait reserved for a special few.

It's a language—spoken in hundreds of beautiful, messy, extraordinary dialects.

And when you celebrate the diversity of how curiosity shows up, you don't just create better conversations.

You create better communities.

Better cultures.

Better possibilities for what we build, heal, imagine, and share next.

Because your curiosity is uniquely yours.

And the world needs it—just as it is.

The Beauty of Different Curiosities

Maybe I'm just blessed.

I grew up in a household where curiosity was praised—where the pursuit of questions, wonderings, and big "What ifs" wasn't just tolerated, it was celebrated.

But as I moved into adulthood—and started spending more of my time around people outside that bubble—I realized something important:

Curiosity doesn't look the same for everyone.

And that's not just okay.

It's beautiful.

Some people ask questions out loud, relentlessly.

Some people wonder quietly, turning things over in their minds for days before they speak.

Some leap. Some linger.

And none of it is wrong.

What lights me up more than anything is seeing people lean into their own brand of curiosity—however it shows up.

When someone asks a thoughtful question instead of making an assumption...

When they stay open when it would be easier to close off...

That's where life happens.

You never really know what people are carrying, what they've lived, or what dreams they hold unless you get curious enough to find out.

And isn't that what this whole book has been about?

Leaning into that superpower.

Not just to become a better leader, creator, or business owner.

But to become a better human.

A more understanding partner.

A more present parent.

A more compassionate neighbor.

A more alive, awake, aware version of yourself.

Life doesn't find its richness in perfect answers.

It finds it in curiosity fully embraced—however it looks for you.

E. Acknowledging the Role of AI and Final Reflections

Before we close, I want to acknowledge something.

This book didn't happen by accident.

It was born from the collision of two powerful forces:

- Human curiosity—the questions I couldn't stop asking, the wonder I refused to quiet, the desire to create something that could meet you where you are.
- AI technology—the tool that helped me organize, refine, and reflect my own thoughts back to me in ways that sparked even deeper inquiry.

It wasn't one or the other.

It was a partnership.

My human heart.

My messy brain.

My imperfect, relentless, passionate curiosity.

And a tool that helped me bring it forward with more clarity, more precision, and yes—more play.

I didn't hand over my voice to AI.

I let it be a sounding board, a co-creator, a mirror that asked me better questions when I needed them most.

And that, more than anything, is what I hope this journey has shown you:

Your curiosity is not a weakness.

It's not a distraction.

It's not childish or naive or impractical.

It's your superpower.

In a world that will try, over and over again, to reward certainty and punish wonder…

You've chosen something braver.

You've chosen to keep asking.

To stay open.

To stay playful.

To stay wild-hearted and awake.

And for that?

I honor you.

I celebrate you.

I thank you.

Thank you for going on this journey.

Thank you for being willing to look at the world—and yourself—with fresh eyes.

Thank you for daring to imagine that your questions are not a problem to be fixed, but a force to be unleashed.

The future belongs to the curious.

And if you've made it to this page,

I know one thing for sure:

You're ready.

About the Author

 Jacqueline "Jax" Crider is a dynamic entrepreneur, financial educator, and visionary leader in the mortgage industry. With a unique blend of legal expertise, financial acumen, and a passion for empowerment, Jax 3 has revolutionized the approach to mortgages and financial education.

As the founder of PBJ Mortgage and Financial Mastery Simplified, Jax has made it her mission to demystify complex financial concepts, making them as accessible as making a peanut butter and jelly sandwich. Her innovative approach, underpinned by the core values of educate, empathize, and empower, has transformed the mortgage experience for countless clients.

Jax's expertise is grounded in a solid educational background, including a law degree and numerous financial certifications. This multidisciplinary knowledge allows her to provide comprehensive, well-rounded guidance to her clients and students.

A prolific educator, Jax is the host of the Financial Mastery Simplified podcast and has amassed over 85,000 views on her YouTube channel. Her first book, "The Secret Sauce of Homebuying," is set for release in November, with a second book, "Ask the Question," already in the works with She Rises Studios.

Jax's commitment to financial education extends beyond her businesses. She actively participates in the Foundation for Choice mentorship program, educating high school students on financial literacy. This aligns with her personal passion for raising strong, financially savvy women, inspired by her role as a mother to a 3-year-old daughter and stepmother to three adult daughters.

In her approach to business and life, Jax emphasizes the importance of intellectual curiosity, continuous learning, and leveraging technology to work smarter, not harder. She's a strong advocate for collaboration among women in the field and uses AI and other modern tools to enhance productivity and reach.

When she's not revolutionizing financial education or mentoring the next generation, Jax enjoys reading, writing, and spending time with her family, including their beloved mascots, Peanut Butter and Jelly. Jax Crider is more than just a mortgage professional; she's a thought leader, an innovator, and a passionate advocate for financial empowerment. Through her various platforms and initiatives, she continues to inspire and educate, helping individuals achieve financial freedom on their own terms.

JOIN THE MOVEMENT: ASK BETTER. LIVE BOLDER. BUILD FREEDOM.

#ASKTHEQUESTION | #PBJWAY | #FINANCIALINSTINCTS

If you made it to this page, here's what I know about you:

You don't want canned advice.
You don't want cookie-cutter money rules.
And you're definitely not interested in doing life on autopilot.

You're the kind of person who thinks, questions, and refuses to accept "that's just how it's done."

That is exactly who this movement is for.

This book was your permission slip.
Your next step is your power move.

You don't need more information — you need the **right conversations and the right questions.** And that's exactly what we've built for you in two simple next steps.

STEP 1 — LISTEN TO THE PODCAST (FREE, HIGH-IMPACT, NO FLUFF)

Your next stop is my show:

🎙 **Financial Mastery Simplified (YouTube)**
https://www.youtube.com/@FinancialMasterySimplifi-vr2wp

This is not your typical money podcast. It's where mindset meets money, neuroscience meets real life, and bold questions replace tired rules.

On the show you'll hear:

- How to trust your financial instincts again
- Why traditional money advice fails smart women
- How to think differently about wealth, confidence, and choice
- Real stories that help you feel seen — not judged

Start with one episode.
Let your brain stretch.
Let your curiosity lead.

You'll walk away thinking differently — and that's the whole point.

STEP 2 – BOOK A CLARITY CALL (WHEN YOU'RE READY TO MOVE)

If homeownership, refinancing, or money clarity is on your mind, the most powerful next step is a real conversation — not a calculator, not a generic form, not a 17-page checklist.

Book your call here:

👉 **pbjteam.com**

On this call, we help you ask the *right questions* before you make big financial decisions. No pressure, no scripts — just clarity and real talk.

We'll help you:

- Cut through mortgage confusion
- Understand your options in plain English
- See what's actually possible for you
- Make decisions that feel aligned — not forced

You don't need to have it all figured out.
You just need to ask the question.

We'll help with the rest.

WHY ACT NOW
(GENTLE URGENCY, REAL IMPACT)

Here's what usually happens after a book like this:

People feel inspired...
Then life gets loud again.

Bills. Emails. Kids. Work. Noise.
And the curiosity fades.

Don't let that be you.

Right now your thinking is open.
Right now new pathways are forming in your brain.
Right now is when change is easiest.

So take **one small step today**:
✓ Listen to one podcast episode
✓ Or book your call at **pbjteam.com**

Momentum begins with a single intentional action.

STAY CONNECTED

Follow along for bold money thinking and smart questions:

Instagram: **@pbj_mortgage**
Facebook: **PBJ Mortgage**
LinkedIn: **Jacqueline (Jax) Crider**

Share your biggest takeaway from this book:
#AskTheQuestion #PBJWay #FinancialInstincts

FINAL INVITATION

This book didn't give you answers.
It trained you to think differently.

Now go use that power.

Ask boldly.
Trust yourself.
Take your next step — your way.

Because the future doesn't belong to people with perfect answers...

It belongs to people who ask better questions.

I'll see you on the podcast — and when you're ready, I'll see you on your clarity call.

—Jacqueline "Jax" Crider
Founder, PBJ Mortgage
Creator, Financial Mastery Simplified

9 781971 349534